Martin Willson was born in England in 1946. After receiving his Ph.D. from the University of Cambridge in 1971, in radioastronomy, he went to Australia and engaged in research in physics for several more years, this time in the field of climatology. Then, realizing the irrelevance of scientific research to the world's greatest problems, he left to explore alternative ways of life. Soon he was living at Chenrezig Institute, a Tibetan Buddhist centre in the Queensland bush, where in 1977 he took ordination as a novice monk. He studied there for three years under Geshe Thubten Lodan and Lama Zasep Tulku, and with their encouragement began to translate texts that were needed for the teaching programme. In 1980 he moved to Tharpa Choeling, Geshe Rabten's centre for Western monks in Switzerland, and now directs Wisdom Publications Dharma Translation Unit (DHATU) in England.

Rebirth and the Western Buddhist

Rebirth and the Western Buddhist

Martin Willson

Wisdom Publications London

First published in 1984
Second edition 1987

Wisdom Publications
23 Dering Street
London W1, England

© Martin Willson 1987

British Cataloguing in Publication Data
Willson, Martin
    Rebirth and the western Buddhist.
    1. Reincarnation (Buddhism)
    2. Title
    294.3'4237   BQ4485

ISBN 0 86171 215 3

Set in Palatino 11 on 13½ by Setrite
and printed and bound by
J. Helen Productions, Hong Kong.

Contents

Contents

Preface to the Second Printing

We are brought up under an ideology that insists there is no truth in the idea of rebirth, but when we come into contact with Buddhist teachings we find that Buddhist tradition has always taken the truth of rebirth as a matter of course, and often lays great stress on it. This clash of incompatible views is a problem for many who for one reason or another feel attracted to Buddhism. Few Westerners can accept without question everything that is taught in one of the great Buddhist traditions, but the opposite extreme of rejecting the teaching of rebirth altogether reduces certain systems of meditation to scattered fragments that do not add up to a coherent method of practice.

This essay examines the subject of rebirth from the point of view of a Western Buddhist with scientific training in seach of the most suitable middle path between these two extremes. It was written at Tharpa Choeling, Switzerland, in 1981–2, for a Buddhist magazine (which in the event never appeared). It is basically what scientists call a review article, not intended as a substitute for reading the more important of the original works, but drawing together salient points from a wide range of literature to show what sort of overall pattern is starting to emerge, despite all the deficiencies and uncertainties of the data so far available.

M.A.G.W.
January 1986

1 Why it is Important to Understand that Rebirth Exists

According to the teachings of Atisha and his successors on the Stages of the Path (*Lam rim*), one becomes a Buddhist and commences the practice of the Buddha-dharma when one takes refuge in the Three Jewels — Buddha, Dharma, and Sangha — with one of three motivations: (1) With horror of rebirth in ill destinies (as an animal, a *preta*, or a hell being), one seeks the aid of the Three Jewels in order to gain "happy" rebirth as a human being, *deva* or *asura*. (2) With horror at the suffering inherent in all states of rebirth under the control of karma and defilements (*kleśa*), one takes refuge in order to achieve liberation from *saṃsāra*, this cycle of death and involuntary rebirth. (3) With infinite great compassion unable to bear the sufferings of any other samsaric being, one takes Refuge in order to become able to lead them all to liberation and enlightenment, for which purpose one must oneself attain the powers of a fully enlightened Buddha.

Not one of these motivations makes sense if one disbelieves in rebirth. Even outside Buddhism, the aim of the Hindu practitioner is liberation (*moksha*), as in the intermediate-level Buddhist motivation — liberation from the cycle of samsaric death and rebirth. As Arnaud Desjardins writes,

> In fact, this Liberation was always defined as escaping from samsara, liberating oneself from

9

the chain of deaths and births, from transmigration. As ninety nine per cent of Europeans do not "believe in reincarnation," considered as an Asiatic superstition, the question was closed: the Hindus and Buddhists consecrate their efforts to liberating themselves from a servitude which does not exist.[1]

If the idea of liberation even for oneself alone is thus meaningless for Westerners, how much more so is the Bodhisattva's goal (3) above — full Enlightenment in order to be able to liberate others. Thus the very essence of religious practice is a concern wider than for this life alone.

Buddhists would generally argue that since, without rebirth, the law of karma and result cannot operate, everything becomes meaningless for the disbeliever in rebirth: our present situation becomes a mere accident, when other beings hurt us it is their fault and not ours, and there is no basis for the practice of morality. This argument should not be pressed too far — it is obvious, in view of the existence of many Christians and others of exemplary conduct despite their disbelief in rebirth, that there are other possible bases for moral behaviour; nevertheless, such examples are rare compared with the confused and misguided behaviour evident all around us, which results from ignorance of the facts of rebirth and karma. Because of this ignorance, the blame for the world's misery is laid on scapegoats and the methods that could actually improve matters are neglected.

Therefore a proper understanding of the fundamental fact of rebirth is necessary as a prerequisite to all Buddhist practice and to overcoming the misery of the world.

This is not to deny that there are also bad reasons for fascination with rebirth. Conze writes of certain "rich old women" whom the doctrine of reincarnation attracts for three reasons, (1) because it allows them to believe that they have spent much of their time in the past as Egyptian princesses and the like, (2) because it frees them from the sense of social guilt which is endemic in the bourgeoisie of the twentieth century, by persuading them that they deserve their money and privileges as a reward for merit gained in the past and (3) because it convinces them that their precious selves will not be lost when they die. In addition theosophy promises them a share in the wisdom of the ages and thrilling participation in mysterious and esoteric kinds of knowledge.[2]

The second misapplication of the rebirth doctrine, to justify social oppression, is of course not confined to Westerners. A proper understanding of rebirth eliminates these errors.

2 *Buddha Taught Rebirth*

Throughout the recorded teachings of the Lord Buddha, from his first sermon at Rishi-patana to His passing away, the doctrine of rebirth is constantly reiterated. Let us take, for example, his account of the meditation under the *bodhi* tree which led to his enlightenment. According to the *Lalitavistara*, in the first watch of the night, having passed progressively through the four *dhyānas*, the Bodhisattva directed his mind to the wisdom-knowledge of the divine eye (*divya-cakshus*), which perceives the passing away and rebirth of sentient beings.

> With His divine eye, perfectly pure and surpassing the human, the Bodhisattva saw sentient beings passing away and being reborn, in good castes and bad castes, good destinies and ill destinies, low and high. He distinguished sentient beings migrating according to their karma: "Alas! These sentient beings have misconduct of body, they have misconduct of speech and mind, they belittle the *Āryas* and hold perverse views. Because of incurring karma with perverse views, when their bodies are destroyed, after death, they are reborn in loss, ill destiny and ruin, in the hells. But these sentient beings have good conduct of body, have good conduct of speech and mind, do not belittle the *Āryas*, and hold right view. Because

of incurring karma with right view, when their bodies are destroyed, they are reborn in a good destiny, in the heavenly worlds."[3]

Then,

> When his mind was thus collected, quite pure, quite clean, clear, without stain, free of minor defilements, supple, serviceable, stable and having attained immovability, in the middle watch of the night the Bodhisattva directed and turned his mind towards the realization of the wisdom-knowledge recollecting previous abodes (*pūrva-nivāsānusmṛiti-jñāna*), and recollected the various previous abodes of Himself and other beings. It was like this: he recollected one birth, two, three, four, five, ten, twenty, ...10^{18} births,...many 10^{18} births; world-ages of destruction, world-ages of arising, world-ages of destruction and arising; and many world-ages of destruction and arising. "There I had such-and-such a name, such was my family, such my caste, such my colour. Such was my food, such was my lifespan, so long did I exist. The pleasures and sufferings I experienced were like this. When I passed away from that existence I was reborn there. Having passed away from there, I was reborn here." Thus with the aspects and with the countries He recollected the various previous abodes of Himself and all sentient beings.[4]

Other accounts of this crucial meditation, in the *Vinaya-vastu*[5] and the Pāli *Vinaya-piṭaka*,[6] differ as to the order and other parts of the meditation, but all include these two sections, in virtually identical words.

These two clairvoyant powers are not confined to the

Bodhisattva; they are also taught in many places (e.g. the *Sāmaññaphala-sutta*[7]) as members of a group of five superknowledges (*abhijñā*), which any practitioner can attain once he has achieved the fourth *dhyāna*.

Rebirth is also frequently mentioned in the sutras when the Buddha explains present events in terms of karma of distant lives, and when he teaches the results of actions and the necessity for practice. For example, in the *Pravrajyāntarāya-sūtra*:

> If, Mahānāma, a householder is given to four modes of behaviour, he [will have to endure] adverse conditions: he will be born again and again, born either blind, dull-witted, dumb, or as an outcaste, always living in misery, always a victim of abuse. He will become a hermaphrodite or a eunuch, or be born into lifelong slavery. He [may also] become a woman, a dog, a pig, an ass, a camel or a poisonous snake, and [thus] be unable to put the Buddha's teachings into practice.[8]

(The four modes are obstructing beings who are bent on following the Path, obstructing the ordination of members of his family, not trusting the holy Dharma, and aversion to virtuous ascetics and brahmins.) Besides rebirth as an animal or a *preta*, numerous sutras of both the Hinayana and Mahayana teach that rebirth in the hells will result from actions ranging from lechery[9] and eating meat[10] to criticising the Perfection of Wisdom.[11]

Furthermore, disbelief in rebirth and in the laws of karma and result are frequently mentioned as wrong views;[12] the classification of *Ārya* beings taught in the *Prajñā-pāramitā-sūtras*[13] involves the number of rebirths they must undergo; and so on. Altogether, rebirth is a virtually inseparable part of Buddhist thinking. It is quite impossible to compress the richness of the Buddhist world-view, with each being evolving through a limitless variety of states over countless aeons, into the impoverished mental frame of those who deny it.

Since amateur writers on Buddhism never tire[14] of making the absurd claim that the teaching of rebirth is somehow contradicted by the principle of Selflessness (*nairātmya*), we should point out that this is a thorough misconception. In the main, as Har Dayal points out,[15] "This difficulty has arisen from the regrettable mistake of translating *ātman* by the English word 'soul.'" Since "soul" means, among other things, "the spiritual part of man regarded as surviving after death and as susceptible of happiness or misery in a future state,"[16] it is hard to see how it could ever have been considered a possible translation for the changeless, partless and independently self-existent *ātman* that the Buddhists deny. Such an *ātman* would be incapable of acting as a soul.[17] The principle of Selflessness negates certain deluded views of *how* such a soul, or anything else included in or imputed upon the aggregates, exists, but certainly does not deny that they exist at all. The nihilistic misinterpretation of Selflessness is the most dangerous of wrong views: "It were better, Kāśyapa, to abide in a personality-view as big as Mount Sumeru, than the emptiness-view of the nihilist."[18] Exactly as my personal continuum follows on from year to year in this life, each moment of my body and mind arising in dependence on the preceding moment, so it follows on from life to life, always changing.

3 Observational Evidence for the Fact of Rebirth

For us, brought up in a cultural milieu decidedly hostile to the idea of rebirth, the statements attributed to the Buddha are unlikely on their own to instil confidence. Perhaps, we may think, he taught that way only because rebirth was the accepted belief at the time, but really meant it to be interpreted as some kind of metaphor. One's misgivings may be considerably allayed by reading Head and Cranston's anthology,[19] which demonstrates the universality of the idea of "reincarnation" and its deep roots in Western as well as Eastern thought. But still, opinions, however reputable and widely held, are hardly enough.

Aware of this, Buddhist pandits of medieval India and their Tibetan successors devoted some energy to providing proofs of rebirth, liberation and other Buddhist doctrines by logical reasoning. Here, however, we come upon one of the major differences between their civilisation and ours: the supposedly rational West has learned to mistrust logical reasoning. The Greek Sophists used it to establish nihilist and other theses, the medieval school-men to establish the existence of God; and now "sophism" and "scholasticism" are used mainly as terms of abuse. The principal propagator of the *Prajñā-pāramitā-sūtras* in our time, no lover of Science, remarks: "I have never paid much attention to logical reasoning, but prefer direct observation,"[20] with which any scientist must agree. Kant too has pointed out that "All cognition of things merely from pure understanding or pure reason is nothing but sheer illusion, and only in experience is there truth."[21] So before approaching the logical "proofs" of rebirth, let us turn now to the observational evidence.

The Western literature on rebirth is vast and rapidly increasing. Here I can give only a brief survey of the types of evidence to be found, referring the reader to the original sources for all the details, which are, of course, indispensable for generating conviction.

One can learn about one or more of one's past lives (1) by recollecting it oneself or (2) by being told about it by another. If one recollects it oneself, it can be (1) spontaneous recall without any training; (2) recall through deliberate training in this or previous lives; or (3) recall under hypnotic regression. In any case, to serve as evidence for rebirth, the recollection needs to be verified in some way to demonstrate that it is not just a fantasy. Even people who have recalled their own past life under hypnosis or otherwise do not necessarily "believe" in rebirth as a result. In hypnotic recall it is common to feel "I must be making all this up."[22]

RECOLLECTING REBIRTH ONESELF

1. *Spontaneous recall*

Spontaneous recall, generally the recollection by a child of his immediately preceding life, and often of how he passed from that death to the present birth, is more common than is often thought. Normally, especially in the West, a young child who talks of its previous life soon learns not to. Doubtless any mother would tend to tire of repeated requests by her child to go "home" to its previous family, perhaps telling her "My own mother is much better than you."[23]

A life spontaneously recalled is generally very recent, so that there are likely to be persons still living who remember the deceased person. In these circumstances, very strong confirmation is often possible.

The child may give much detailed information on his former family and home, often not very far away but unknown to his present family, which can be confirmed by visiting the past-life abode. If the child comes on such a visit (as he is generally eager to do), he recognises places, buildings, and people known to him in his former life, and his former possessions, comments on changes since he was there, asks after missing possessions and old acquaintances, and so on. His intimate knowledge convinces his widow, say, that he is indeed her deceased husband. He may give details of debts outstanding at the time of his death, including ones unknown to his surviving former relatives, which are subsequently confirmed. If he died by violence (which apparently makes quick rebirth and spontaneous recall more probable[24]), he may give details of his murder which can be confirmed from police records and witnesses.

A child who claims to have lived in a foreign country often exhibits behavioural traits, food preferences etc. appropriate to that country. He may display skills which there has been no opportunity to learn in the present life, such as speaking a language unknown to anyone in his community,[25] or being able to perform very intricate Indian dances at a very early age, consistent with the claimed previous life as a dancer in India.[26]

There can also be other circumstantial evidence supporting the child's claim. If he was known to his new mother in his previous life, she may well have had a significant dream or vision of his coming to her, before his birth. Someone else too may have a dream to the same effect. The child may carry birthmarks resembling and in the same place as the wounds which caused his previous death, or even reproducing a mark deliberately applied to his predecessor's body to enable identification if he should be reborn in that family. As many as 300 of the cases investigated bore such marks or congenital malformations.[27]

Some 1600 cases of spontaneous recall in various parts of the world, including 241 in Europe,[27] have been investigated with great thoroughness by Dr. Ian Stevenson[28] of the University of Virginia. This work provides the strongest scientific evidence for rebirth that we yet have—anyone of a scientific turn of mind who still doubts the reality of rebirth should definitely read some of the reports of it, in full. The above examples of the types of evidence found are taken from the book by the English Buddhist Francis Story,[29] who co-operated with Stevenson in Sri Lanka, Thailand and India—the book largely responsible for persuading the present author that the materialist view denying life beyond death was incorrect.

Some of these phenomena are also reported in connection with Tibetan Rinpoches or incarnate lamas, but without investigation by persons with scientific training.[29a] What Westerners can attest is the remarkable precocity of the young rinpoches, a feature also noted in many of Stevenson's and Story's cases.

2.   *Recall through deliberate training*

Recall through deliberate training can occur through the practice of meditation in the present life. As indicated above, according to the Buddha's teaching, the super-knowledge of recollecting previous lives can be attained through practising concentration until perfect Calm Abiding (*śamatha*) is realised—nine stages are distinguished in this process[30]—then going on to develop the four absorptions (*dhyāna*). This may be expected to take years of retreat devoted entirely to this practice, in conditions of quiet and isolation that Mara[31] has succeeded in almost eliminating from the Western world. The yogin who achieves it also has access to such magical powers as levitation, invisibility, multiplying the body, and passing unobstructed through walls or mountains,[32] whose rarity these days needs no stressing. Before one can even start, one must (according to Tibetan teaching) have practised thoroughly the meditations of the Stages of the Path (*Lam rim*), which themselves demand faith in rebirth, karma and other doctrines as a prerequisite. So this is not a way for sceptics to persuade themselves they have lived before.

The American scientist Dr. John Lilly[33,34] has reported acquiring the power of past-life recall during his explorations of states of consciousness, but apparently regards it as of no significance and gives no details. His techniques include the use of an isolation tank specially designed to eliminate normal sensory stimuli. It could well be that we have to look to some such device if *dhyāna* is to be practicable in the West.

There are a very few persons who develop with comparatively little effort the faculty of recalling past lives in great detail, known in England as "far memory." This is quite different from the spontaneous recall discussed above, since the lives recalled are much more remote, the faculty is recovered only in adult life, and the recall includes recollection of having trained in meditational practices relevant to far memory many lives before. The outstanding example is Joan Grant, who recalls having trained for ten years to develop far memory when she was Princess Sekeeta in First-dynasty Egypt, and as a result of that training retains the ability, and other psychic gifts, even now.[35] She has told the story of several of her past lives in a series of books published as novels. Those I have been able to find[36-39] (especially the first,[36] on her life as Sekeeta) are pervaded by an extraordinary brightness and clarity of vision, each everyday detail, such as a children's game, alive and beautiful. Egyptologists found the details amazingly accurate.[40] Even if these books were the outcome of painstaking historical research, they would establish their author as a person of an altogether exceptional depth of compassionate understanding. But in fact they were dictated in a sort of trance state in a series of fragments over whose order the author had no control, but which fitted together perfectly when rearranged; and Joan Grant had not made any study of Egyptology.[35] Her series of births in the Egyptian royal family and nobility, sometimes as a man and sometimes a woman, was entirely appropriate to her continuing work for others: she is decidedly not one of the blatant fantasists to whom Conze's remark quoted above refers. During this life she works in London with her husband, the psychiatrist Dr. Denys Kelsey, treating those with problems rooted in previous existences.[41]

Another case of far memory is the yoga teacher Elisabeth Haich, also trained as a princess in ancient Egypt, but rather differently.[42] It is quite possible that, as she claims, the genetic endowment of the early Egyptian royalty, besides resulting in the physical characteristics observable in their statues and mummies, also involved a particular aptitude for spiritual practice. We shall return to her in Chapter Six.

Other authors have also claimed to have written books by far memory. The only one I have read is Guirdham's *The Island*,[43] set in Greece around 1300 BC. In isolation, it is unlikely to convince the sceptic that it was not compiled from readily obtainable historical information and sexual fantasies. Perhaps it is more credible when combined with his other works.

In non-Buddhist traditions, there exist methods by which less advanced students can gain some recall of incidents from their recent previous existences. The late Swami Prajñanpad of Bengal employed such a technique[44] to relieve his Western disciples (or rather, "candidate-disciples") of the strongest impressions from previous lives that obstructed their practice. It is somewhat like psychoanalysis, involving a skilled therapist and a single student in many hours of concentrated effort, working back from present emotions to relive the most agonising and deeply repressed moments of the student's past until the key emotional block hidden in each is revealed and then overcome. This method is now practised in France by the Swami's disciples, Arnaud and Denise Desjardins.[45,46] Mme. Desjardins' book,[46] describing twenty of the French cases, gives fascinating insight into how past-life experiences affect our present existence. Of eighty-eight persons who had undergone the process in depth, seventy-three recovered previous lives, many of the other fifteen still being beginners.[47]

The purpose of this effort is not to provide evidence for rebirth: no attempt is made to recall names or dates, and the chances of any past-life event turning up that could be traced in historical records is remote. (Nevertheless, Mme Desjardins' moving account of her own past-life recall[44] mentions that her dramatic meeting with Śrī Mā Anandamayī at the end of her previous existence has twice been confirmed by the latter in front of witnesses.) But traumas both of the present life (such as the birth experience) and evidently not of the present life (such as death experiences) are relived similarly, and it is seen that while details of the former can often be verified by the subject's parents, the latter are certainly not of less emotional importance to the subject. If the past-life event recalled were merely a fantasy, why should it be felt as so overwhelmingly important, why should it explain the subject's present character so well, and why should working on it have such beneficial effects? In fact, it is often found that the birth or early childhood experience of the present life itself involved a (subconscious?) recall of a past-life experience, which was responsible for the powerful effect. For example, a certain baby, placed in his cradle in such a way that he cannot move his arms, finds this particularly unbearable because of the echo of his preceding death experience when he was pegged to the ground and left to die.[48] Why too should a fantasy be so realistic and consistent? Why, if the subject is merely acting out an imagined death agony, should he reproduce it *identically* each time, like a film being replayed?[49] On investigation, any explanation other than rebirth becomes very hard to sustain.

3.   *Recall under hypnotic regression*

This is much the most widely-applicable method of investigating previous lives and is now producing spectacular results. It first caught the public attention in 1956 when Morey Bernstein, an American businessman and amateur hypnotist, published *The Search for Bridey Murphy*,[50] which became a best-seller. Having read of the experiments of the English psychiatrist Sir Alexander Cannon in regressing subjects to before their birth, he tried the experiment himself on his best subject, who went back to a life as an Irish woman in the last century. His book includes transcripts of the hypnotic sessions, which show the method clearly. Many of the details elicited from her were subsequently established, with considerable effort, as historically accurate, although Bridey herself was an ordinary, obscure person of whom no specific record was found. The public reaction and the distortions eventually used to discredit the story in defence of Christian and psychoanalytic orthodoxy are described by Cerminara.[51]

Now, past-life regression has become a commonplace. It is routinely applied by hypnotherapists to treat various psychological problems: when hypnotised and asked to go back to the origin of their problem, many patients go back to a previous life. Techniques apparently vary considerably: that of Denys Kelsey and Joan Grant appears almost as arduous as the Desjardins' method discussed above, and by Pisani's account[52,53] produces results of comparable interest. Fiore[54] must be more typical: she makes it sound amazingly easy and seems to manage with hardly more than one or two sessions per patient. Since the object of therapy is to cure the patient, not to collect evidence, there is very little verification in these cases. Fiore adduces the same two arguments as the Desjardins in favour of the reality of the past-life recall: (1) that the subjects cannot be attempting to deceive because no-one could act that well; and (2) that remission of symptoms occurs with regression to a past life just as with regression to an event in the current life, which is often verified by relatives.

Besides these arguments, two means can be used to verify past-life regressions, which almost always are to periods beyond living memory so that the verification methods applied to spontaneous recall are unavailable. Firstly, one can select individual cases and search historical records for confirmation of the details recalled. Secondly, one can apply statistical tests to a large sample.

Until recently, the vast majority of people (like Bridey Murphy) lived and died leaving no written record of their names. Without newspapers, radio or television, they generally knew little of what was going on elsewhere. Therefore to find a case where one can hope for specific historical confirmation, one must hypnotise many subjects and make many past-life regressions to find a few exceptional ones with checkable information. The chance of finding someone who was himself prominent in history is very remote (though Wambach[55] turned up a mid-nineteenth-century President of the United States—a remarkable fluke even in a sample of 1100 cases); but finding someone who was connected with a prominent individual, perhaps as a servant, is quite possible. The principle of verification (just as with "far memory" cases) is that (1) all the information given by the hypnotised subject is consistent with historical sources, (2) some of it is positively confirmed by these sources, and (3) the confirmed information is sufficiently obscure that it is highly unlikely the subject could have learned it in this life. If the subjects give some information not known to historians at the time but later confirmed, this is further evidence that they did not learn it through normal channels—but of course such good fortune is unlikely to come the investigator's way. Nevertheless, Iverson,[56] investigating by this method a series of past-life recalls by a British hypnotist, found a case where the subject, as a Jew in medieval York, hid in the crypt of a certain church in an unsuccessful attempt to escape a massacre: when he checked, that church was held to have no crypt, but soon afterwards the blocked-off crypt was discovered by accident.

The statistical approach has only just become practicable, owing to improvements in technique. Wambach[57] developed a very efficient method in which the subjects are not required to speak under hypnosis, but are told to remember everything vividly and discuss it when awake. Not only does that make it easier to gain information on past lives, so that she was able to elicit past-life memories from as many as ninety percent of her subjects, but by getting the subjects to fill in a written questionnaire she could work with groups of even fifty or more subjects[58] instead of one at a time, and also save all the labour of transcribing tapes. Thus she was able to collect 1088 reports of the past lives of modern Americans, sampled at a series of specified times over the past 4000 years. The reports included the answers to standard questions such as the sex of the subject in the previous life, social status, country, colour, age at death, cause of death, sort of food eaten, utensils used, clothes and footwear worn, and so on. The questions had to be repeated word-for-word with each group of subjects since hypnotised subjects interpret instructions very literally: rather like changing a punctuation mark in a computer program, a seemingly trivial change in wording can generate a great change in response. The resulting statistics allow of many checks not hitherto possible. For example, regardless of the present sex of the subjects, their sex distribution in past lives was almost exactly fifty-fifty; and the class distribution (judged from the quality of clothes worn etc.) showed definitely that most past lives recalled were of poor and humble status and the percentage of upper-class rebirths was realistically small. If the recalls were fantasies one would perhaps expect a preponderance of upper-class, male lives. The other data collected were virtually all consistent within the sample, and realistic compared with historical information. For example, many subjects reported dying in infancy, and it is hard to see why anyone would fantasise such a life. One can be sure too that in fantasies there would be numerous anachronisms regarding the clothing, food and utensils. Food at most past periods was notably dreary. Whereas the past-life regressions of patients who come to psychiatrists with phobias and sexual problems show a high percentage of violent deaths and gruesome rapes, as one finds in Fiore's book[54] for example, this much more representative sample of past lives shows only eighteen percent of violent deaths. Particularly interesting is the curve showing the fraction of present-day Americans alive at various past time periods,which well reflects the increase in world population from 500 AD on. This has significant implications for Buddhist dogma, which I shall consider below. The study also investigated experiences in the intermediate state,[59] with considerable religious relevance.

Wambach's research is an impressive break-through, which could well have far-reaching effects as the work is repeated in other countries and further refined. If her results are confirmed, it is inevitable that such data will eventually come to be recognised as valid for archaeological and historical purposes and give us a much more complete picture of the history of humankind. Vanished peoples, who have left no physical trace for archaeologists, yet survive in these memories. So does the knowledge and experience accumulated over millennia by so-called "primitive" peoples whom our "civilisation" has thoughtlessly wiped out, including the important point of what it actually felt like to live in those societies. It is clear that a lot of people are very interested in the knowledge of themselves that these hypnotic techniques can bring, and no exceptional abilities are needed to become an amateur hypnotist and try them out.[59a] Thus there is every prospect that the experience of past lives could become widespread, and many attitudes are likely to change as a result.

BEING TOLD ABOUT ONE'S PAST LIVES BY ANOTHER

This includes two cases, depending whether (1) the other recognises you as a person he or she knew in a previous life, or (2) he or she has the general psychic power of perceiving anyone's previous lives, as described in Chapter Two. The first is by far the more common.

1.   *Recognition from previous lives*

This is about as common as people remembering their own previous lives, since people associated in past lives frequently come together again in this life. A husband and wife are likely to have been in the same relationship before, or the other way round, or brother and sister, or mother and son, etc., and likewise with less close relationships. Examples abound in all the sources of information available to us, from Sūtras to modern hypnotic cases. For example, Wambach[57] included a question on this in her survey. Obviously, if you recall your own past

life by hypnosis or otherwise and recognise someone
now known to you in it, you can tell him; but he will not
necessarily understand.

So one need not be too surprised when an English
psychiatrist, Dr. Guirdham, is recognised by one of his
patients, a Mrs. Smith, as having been her lover in the
Languedoc in the thirteenth century.[60] Mrs. Smith's
flashes of far memory come mainly in dreams, and provide a string of names of persons and places, and recollections of events. What is most remarkable about this case
is the extent of the historical confirmation which Guirdham managed to find. Despite the lapse of seven centuries, the existence of many of the persons named is
established from the records of the Inquisition; for they
were Cathars, many of whom were interrogated and
imprisoned or executed. An event which for years had
haunted the dreams of both Guirdham and Smith is
identified as the massacre of the Inquisitors at Avignonet
on 28 May 1242, which is well documented.[61] Some of this
success in historical research is apparently due to "discarnate entities" who helped Guirdham to look in the
right place. The story expands with the help of several
psychic friends of Guirdham, the discarnate entities
(often the same friends after their decease), and the
recovery of his own faculty of far memory, to fill several
books and build up a picture of a group of twenty-odd
people, members of which have been reborn together on
at least seven occasions, apparently in order to practise
healing and to disseminate the "Dualist" ideas taught by
the Cathars.[61a] Guirdham may well be effective as a
healer, but his expositions of Catharism carry surprising-
ly little conviction for one who claims to have been the
favourite disciple of Guilhabert de Castres, most famous
of Cathar teachers, to converse with him in visions, and
to be writing at his request.[61b] That the priestess in *The
Island*, one of the wisest of the group, should say that to

learn quickly of one's past lives "is almost always a disaster", and "to tear at the curtains which divide us from the past is always evil,"[62] is also puzzling when the sources described above show that recalling past lives is often strikingly beneficial. As suggested above, some readers may find the bizarre adventures Guirdham reports in this book a little hard to believe; they will not necessarily be reassured by his summary of his other works in *The Middle Way*,[63] disingenuously titled "Clinical Evidence of Reincarnation."

2. *Universal Insight into others' previous lives*

This seems to be a much rarer and more advanced accomplishment than insight into one's own. It is associated particularly with that remarkable being, Edgar Cayce, born in Kentucky in 1877. The following extremely condensed outline of his work is based on the standard account by Cerminara,[64,65] which anyone interested in rebirth should read.

Cayce's astonishing clairvoyant insight into illnesses came to light when he sought the aid of a hypnotist for his own throat ailment. It was soon found that while under hypnosis he could diagnose and prescribe cures for not only his own illness, but also those of others, using medical language unknown to him when awake, and that these cures were frequently successful even when the patient was someone hundreds of miles away whom Cayce had never met and of whom he was told no more than the name and address. Before long, Cayce was devoting his entire life to this work for the relief of suffering. The interest for us lies in that while many illnesses had physical causes, for some Cayce said that the cause lay in the actions of a past life, and that the person must work to extinguish that karma, often by way of spiritual practice. The first such mention of reincarna-

tion and karma, apparently contrary to his Catholic con-
victions, deeply shocked Cayce when he awoke from
trance, but he continued his work when persuaded that
nothing in the Bible actually contradicted it. From 1923 to
his death in 1945, he gave some 2500 "life readings," in
which he was specifically asked to describe the karmic
forces operating in an individual and the past lives in
which they were created. Such readings on newborn
infants accurately predicted their character traits and
aptitudes, as did those on adults, and accounted for them
plausibly by way of the past-life experiences. They were
found helpful by those who followed the advices. The
readings were always consistent with each other—readings on the same individual taken years apart agreed
exactly, and background information on particular times
and places always agreed between different readings,
and was also consistent with historical records where
these exist. Sometimes Cayce indicated where records of
a previous existence could be found, and these were
confirmed. Life readings on Cayce himself indicated that
he had been a high priest in Egypt, with great occult
powers, who fell through self-will and sensuality. His
present life was an opportunity to redeem his past errors
by serving human beings selflessly; which, indeed, he
did, by all accounts.[66]

While much of the information in Cayce's life readings
is quite comparable with what can be gained through
hypnotic regression of the subject, it has greater depth
because of Cayce's direct insight into karma. It is notice-
able that the past lives mentioned by Cayce are, on
average, more ancient than those selected in hypnother-
apy or found by the Desjardins' students; and while the
latter illustrate a rather obvious aspect of karma, the
tendency of mental habits to continue from one life to the
next, Cayce is concerned also with the karmas that determine physical characteristics of the body, such as being

born blind. These, it seems, mature often after thousands of years. It is quite clear that the power of perceiving karma is distinct from that of perceiving past lives, as the Buddha's account in Chapter Two implies. Cayce himself said he drew the information on past lives not only from the individual's "unconscious" mind, but from the "Akashic records" (Skt. *ākāśa*: space) or "Universal Memory of Nature". Conceivably a normal hypnotised subject has access only to the former. In any case, Cayce may well be the first person since the Buddha to give so much information on karma, and as we know that the readings refer to real people of our own time and they are much less of a strain on one's credulity than many of the Buddha's, they are of absorbing interest to any Buddhist.

4 Logical "Proofs": the Theory of Rebirth

When they seek to persuade students of the truth of rebirth, Tibetan lamas do not lean heavily on the observational evidence summarised above, but rely mainly on supposed proofs by logical reasoning. We may instance the widely read books by His Holiness the Dalai Lama[67] and Lama Zopa Rinpoche.[68] On encountering such concise presentations of the standard Buddhist arguments for rebirth, Western students often react with incredulity that intelligent men could expect them to accept such manifest illogic as some of the arguments contain. It is worthwhile to look into the reasons for this failure of communication. Close study of the arguments does not make them much more convincing by Western standards, but can give us some appreciation of why they are put forward.

We are fortunate that a prominent Tibetan logician, the Venerable Losang Gyatso (LG), principal of the Buddhist School of Dialectics at Dharamsala, has recently published an unusually full account[69] of the logical arguments in favour of rebirth. Having been checked by the Dalai Lama, it may be taken as authoritative. I have translated the relevant chapter, and here pick out the important points from its hundred pages of argument, adding my own critical comments, mainly from a scientific viewpoint. In the succeeding chapter, I shall enlarge on the reasons why Westerners find the arguments hard to accept.

33

Reasoning does not take place in a vacuum, but in the context of a theory that provides something to reason about and something to reason from. In Mathematics or Science, a theory starts with basic assumptions—axioms and postulates—supplemented by definitions, which enable deductions to be made. It is considered important to identify the assumptions clearly. In Buddhist philosophy, postulates are not identified as such: anything a proponent of a system would accept is an "assertion," but the assertions are not independent. Challenged to prove assertion A, he may derive it from assertion B. Challenged to prove B, he could well derive it from A. He is not required to present his whole system at once as a sequence of deductions but only to answer questions on one point at a time. Losang Gyatso, however, begins with a series of assertions that we may regard as postulates, P1 to P4. We shall have occasion to recall George Spencer-Brown's definition:

> We may take a postulate to be a statement which is accepted without evidence, because it belongs to a set of such statements from which it is possible to derive other statements which it happens to be convenient to believe. The chief characteristic which has always marked such statements has been an almost total lack of any spontaneous appearance of truth.[70]

> P1: Effective things are not mere conceptual imputations but exist in their own nature, reversed from, or lacking the nature of, other things. (LG 11−12, quoting *Pramāṇavārttika* I.40, which I have interpreted with the standard commentary and Geshe Rabten's explanation.)

Anyone versed in Prāsaṅgika-mādhyamika philosophy or modern physics can see that this is not strictly true. But since it is embarrassing to perform logical analysis on things that are in fact not findable on logical analysis, it is postulated that we are dealing with findable things. In many ways these hypothetical findable things behave much like things in the observed world, so the theory can still be useful. But just as the Newtonian theory of dynamics, which assumes absolute time and space, breaks down when very high velocities are involved, so this theory too may cease to apply in certain circumstances. While this postulate may appear to be about individual things, in practice it is taken to mean that each *type* of thing has numberless defining characteristics, which mark it off from every thing not of that type. This gives rise to the important concept of a *homogene* (*rigs 'dra*): a homogene of A is something that is of the same type as A.

> P_2: A person is a dependent imputation on the aggregates. There is no person self-sufficient or standing up on its own. (LG 12–18, 100)

These first two postulates are consistent with Sautrāntika tenets. The next two form the basis of the theory of causation.

> P_3: Whatever result is produced must be preceded by the complete collection of however many causes it has. If any of them is absent, they are unfit; if one cause is incomplete, that result cannot arise. (LG 21)
>
> P_3': Conversely, if the collection of causes is complete, the result must be produced. (LG 56–57)

> P_4: The complete collection of causes of any result includes (1) the substantial cause (*upādāna*) and (2) co-operative conditions.

"Substantial cause of result R" means "That which leaves

that outcome in the manner of passing into the nature of result R, from itself changing into the other nature" (LG 87). Another definition, found in the Dü-ra, is "Principal producer of R in its own substantial continuum."[71] For example: (1) a lamp[-flame] is the substantial cause of lamplight since "(a) without its nature changing, it cannot become and appear in the nature of the lamplight; and (b) it leaves an outcome in the nature of the lamplight;" (LG 87) (2) the substantial cause of a clay pot is the lump of clay, since that cannot become the nature of the pot without changing; (3) the substantial cause of a rice plant is the grain of rice from which it grows. The earth, manure, heat and moisture assembled together with it, and the farmer, are its co-operative conditions.

Co-operative conditions are also called "dominant conditions" (*adhipati-pratyaya*), and may be divided further into common and uncommon dominant conditions.

This twofold classification of causes and conditions has the advantage over more detailed classifications of being clear-cut and non-redundant: any cause of R is either substantial cause of R or dominant condition of R, and whatever is substantial cause or dominant condition of R is a cause of R.

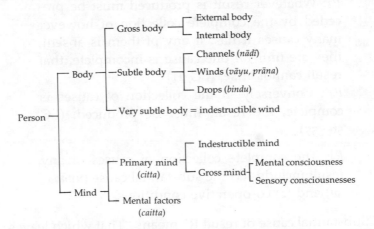

Bases of imputation of the person, after Losang Gyatso.

To apply this theory to the person, the bases of imputation of the person are divided as shown above. The
external body is the material aggregate of flesh and bones
(except for certain miraculously-born beings who possess
a rainbow-light body instead). The internal body is the
five sense faculties. The subtle body is the physical support of the mind, somewhat analogous to the nervous
system in Western physiology. Primary consciousness is
carried by the psychic winds in the system of channels
and channel-chakras—ten types of wind are listed (LG
43–46), with different functions such as enabling bodily
movements and sensory perception:

> Just as a crippled man with vision can go about
> with the support of a blind man who has legs,
> so the primary consciousness, which has the
> ability to perceive objects but not to move
> about, and the winds, which have no ability to
> perceive objects but do have the power to move
> or go, can perform all the functions of appre-
> hending and relating to objects when they as-
> sist each other in mutual support. (LG 44)

Thus from this point of view the channels may be compared to our nerves and the winds to the electrochemical
impulses they transmit. But channels also conduct blood
and "drops"—white drops and red drops, i.e. semen and
that blood which is considered to be the female gene-
rative fluid. The white and red drops received from the
parents at conception remain throughout life in the cavity
at the centre of the heart chakra, where they house the
very subtle, indestructible wind and mind. They also
grow and produce more drops, which collect in the other
chakras.

The indestructible wind and mind, in this system,
which is derived from Anuttara-yoga-tantra texts, exist
continuously, mutually inseparable, their natures un-
changing, regardless of the birth and death of the person,

and are not to be destroyed by any conditions whatever. (LG 50) Thus a concrete answer is given to the perennially puzzling question, "What passes from life to life?" Lo-sang Gyatso claims that the indestructible wind and mind are what is taught in the Sutras under such names as *ālayavijñāna* and *sugata-garbha*, i.e. *tathāgata-garbha* or Buddha-potential. Both these, of course, have been compared to the Hindu concept of *ātman*, and it is hard not to see a certain similarity in the present case also.[72]

Apart from the indestructible wind and mind, which are independent of other causes,[73] all the constituents of the person have their respective substantial cause and dominant condition. We list them for the case of birth from a womb.

The substantial cause of the external body and the channels is the mixed drops of white and red elements obtained from the father and mother respectively.

> The principal substantial cause of the flesh, blood, skin, etc. is the red drop obtained from the mother, while that of the channels, bones, marrow, heart and so on is the white drop obtained from the father. (LG 22)

The dominant condition is karma, mind and the subtle-wind-body produced simultaneously with that mind (LG 24), i.e. the indestructible wind and mind and the karmic imprints they carry.

The substantial causes of the sense faculties and the winds are the impressed potentials of their previous homogenes, existing on the indestructible wind. The common dominant condition of the sense faculties is the parents' semen and blood, and the uncommon dominant condition the consciousness produced together with the previous wind-body. The dominant condition of the winds is likewise the external and internal bodies.

The drops come from the parents.

The substantial cause of each type of mind is its own previous homogene, or the habit thereof. The uncommon dominant condition of the visual consciousness is the visual faculty, (and the common dominant condition the mental faculty[74]); similarly for the other sensory consciousnesses. The uncommon dominant condition of the mental consciousness is the aggregate of volition generated by the actions of will established on previous mental consciousness (LG 85). The body is also a dominant condition of later mental consciousness (LG 86).

This, then, is Losang Gyatso's theoretical model of the birth of a person from the womb. It is hardly excessively complicated, given the complexity of a human being, and not without elegance. From the model, proof of rebirth follows immediately. Any of the constituents, except the drops, has a cause which depends on the previous continuum of the person. By P3, therefore, birth must be preceded by a previous continuum of the person.

So much for the easy part. The hard part, of course, is to establish that this model is realistic. One does not have to establish it all since the argument from any one constituent suffices to establish rebirth, but even so the task is daunting when we consider that the subtle and very subtle bodies appear rather fanciful to most of us, and many in the West even deny that there is a mind apart from the operations of the central nervous system. Note that just making rebirth seem plausible is no use: the object is to establish it in our minds with one hundred percent certainty so that we can start meditation on the Stages of the Path.

Let us analyse the two main arguments, based on the external body and the mind respectively.

1. *Proof based on the external body*

The crucial step here is demonstrating that the body

cannot be produced from material causes alone. Losang Gyatso gives two arguments, both invalidated by scientific observation.

(a) The theory asserts that the substantial cause of the external body of a womb-born being is semen from the father and blood from the mother. Sometimes a misleading impression of modernity is given by translating "semen and blood" as "sperm and egg," but it should be remembered that Tibetans had no idea of the existence of these microscopic germ cells, let alone of how each one holds enough genetic information to fill a whole library of books, as is now well-established by a multitude of observations. Thus it is purely from ignorance of the processes of reproduction that Losang Gyatso is led to argue that the mere combination of semen and blood is insufficient to generate the aggregate called a body because "much semen and blood is seen which even though combined is unable to generate such an aggregate." (LG 24) This simply does not apply to the formation of a body from the fusion of germ cells as understood scientifically, any more than it does to the growth of a plant body via a seed, which in fact involves a closely similar process of fusion of male and female germ cells.

(b) The other argument, to which Losang Gyatso attaches considerable weight, depends on the ancient view that insects and other small creatures are born "from heat, moisture, earth, manure and so on" by spontaneous generation. If there were no need to have the subtle mind and wind-body from a previous existence present as a dominant condition, then all sorts of such creatures would be born in every portion of matter all the time, because the only cause necessary would be the presence of matter (LG 28–35, 56–61).

> There'd be no portion of earth and so on
> In which beings would not be born
> Of heat and moisture and the rest.[75]

While the idea of spontaneous generation seems a laughable superstition to us now, we should remember it was widely held in Europe until the mid-eighteenth century, and for micro-organisms survived until decisively disproved by the work of Pasteur and others.

> Virgil, in his Georgics, gives a recipe for creating bees from a calf. It involves beating the unfortunate calf to death without breaking the skin, in a room with windows facing north, south, east and west. Somewhat later, Van Helmont [(1577–1644)] gave us a formula by which mice could be obtained from grains of wheat and a dirty undergarment.[76]

It is now known that all the insects and small creatures to which Tibetans attribute birth by spontaneous generation[77] are in fact born from eggs, produced by parents. Anyone can confirm this by careful observation. As for fossils, which Tibetans imagine to be the remains of animals born spontaneously inside rock through some terrible karma, where they pass a miserable existence in darkness and solitude, unable to move, we now understand how the remains of animals who lived quite normally on the surface of the earth can become encased in rock subsequently, and the Tibetan explanation is rejected as in conflict with numerous observations. The argument thus collapses as there is no reason to believe spontaneous generation exists at all. If it occurred long ago, at the origin of life on Earth, that was through numerous extremely unlikely conditions coming together, and thus does not validate Losang Gyatso's argument. As yet, Buddhists have not offered any more satisfactory explanation of that event than anyone else.

Losang Gyatso also asserts that *Āryas* directly perceive the subtle (i.e. "indestructible") wind and mind (p. 35). Without more information—does this come from actual statements by persons recognised as *Āryas*, or is it merely theoretical? If the former, were they perhaps Tantric yogins who had spent years deliberately trying to visualise those things?—it is of no evidential value.

Thus the proof of previous lives based on the external body is unestablished, unless perhaps you happen to be an *Ārya*, in which case you do not need it.

2. *Proof based on the mind*

This is clearly the most important proof, being the one given by all three Tibetan authors. In its simplest syllogistic form, the argument to be substantiated is:

> With respect to the knowing of an ordinary
>   being just born:
>   it is preceded by earlier knowing;
>   because it is knowing.[78]

"Knowing" is synonymous with consciousness, or mind, according to Lo-rig texts. The Buddhist assertions are that (1) mind exists as an effective (impermanent) thing (therefore it must have causes), and (2) the causes of any mind cannot be wholly material, but must include an earlier mind of the same type in the same personal continuum. The denial of either or both of these propositions is termed *materialism*. There were various different materialist views even in ancient India, where the materialists (*Lokāyatas*) were a small, eccentric minority, and there are more today when forms of materialism are the established orthodoxy in much of the world. The problem of "mind and matter" has been a source of much controversy among philosophers both Buddhist and non-Buddhist for millennia, and continues to be disputed vigorously by biologists, physicists, parapsychologists, philosophers and others. Any claim to have established a unique solution by simple logic is therefore going to face many objections.

Accepting proposition (1) just for the moment, we can seek to establish (2) either directly or by eliminating the various materialist views one by one. Direct establishment involves noting that one's present mental experiences come in a continuum or succession of mental states and include memories of one's past experiences in this life, and persuading oneself that it is inconceivable it could ever have been otherwise. It would seem that if one understánds the nature of mind, one sees it *has* to be so; just as with God, according to St. Anselm:

> No one who understands what God is can conceive that God does not exist.[79]

It seems to me unlikely that one could attain such depth of understanding without coming on direct traces of one's previous existences, which would render the syllogistic proof superfluous. In any case, for those without such understanding, the refutations of the materialist views are given.

According to the Tibetan commentaries, the Indian materialists offered at least three ways in which the mind could rely on the body, being produced with it and ceasing with it at death:

> It is the substantial result of the body, like the light of a lamp[-flame?]; or a quality of the body, like beer and the taste of beer; or the special dominant result of the body, like a wall and a painting on the wall. (LG 83)

These are to be considered separately.

(a) Losang Gyatso claims:

> Anything that is gross body cannot act as special dominant condition for the mental consciousness because whatever is help or harm to those bodies does not alone become help or harm to the mental consciousness, and

because the youth or decline of the body does
not bring about youth or decline of the mental
consciousness. (p. 84)

Neither reason appears established, since interference
with the brain (e.g. with electrodes) can certainly affect
the mental consciousness, and mental changes with age
are evident to all. Thus it is hard to see what he means.

(b) That the whole body does not act as substantial
cause of the mind seems obvious at first sight since it
would mean that the whole body turned into mind, thus
disappearing. But as the example of the lamplight suggests, the process of conversion could be imperceptibly
slow, with the material body being replenished by food
etc. before it became apparent. Indeed, the operation of
the nervous system consumes chemical energy which
eventually must come from food, and one might point to
this as just such a process. The Dalai Lama offers the
following consequences in refutation:

> With the development or decline of the body,
> the mind would necessarily be subject to the
> same processes. Further, mind could appear in
> a corpse (since according to materialist views,
> mind is but a function of the elements.)[80]

Losang Gyatso adds:

> It would follow that a sage (*ṛṣhi*) engaging in
> ascetic practices would have a weakened mind;
> ...or else it would follow that just as a wea-
> kening of the body's warmth acts as a substan-
> tial cause for developing a cold sickness, so the
> weakening of the body would act as a cause
> developing the intelligence. (p. 89)

One is struck by the crudity of the alleged consequences,
which ignore all the complexities that must be involved

and lack any attempt to show that they actually do follow from the opponents' positions, or that the predicted effect would be large enough to detect. Losang Gyatso is so unsure what actually follows that he draws two mutually contradictory consequences. Furthermore the consequences are not particularly unacceptable, considering that (1) development of children's intelligence as they grow, and senility, are widely observed; (2) even if one discounts the many Tibetan stories of corpses rising, there are Western reports of people resuscitated after clinical death; and (3) both Lord Buddha and Jetsun Milarepa found nourishing food strengthened their minds for meditation after long fasting.

It is also argued that nothing material can be substantial cause of the mind because mind is formless, and what is form cannot become formless or vice versa.[67,68] This generalisation of assertion (2) (that the causes of any mind cannot be wholly material, but must include an earlier mind of the same type in the same personal continuum) is likely to be greeted still more suspiciously by those of other schools, who will be justifiably wary of what interpretation the Buddhist might put on the words, and to whom it looks like an arbitrary dogma. Physicists have shown light is a form of energy interconvertible with others, including matter, so why should not mind, which the Buddhists themselves say is "clear light," be interconvertible with matter too? Cannot a yogin create a new body mentally, and manifest all manner of material objects purely by power of the mind? Ultimately, are not all dharmas of the same nature, Voidness? What do "form" and "formless" mean in relation to Einstein's demonstration that matter itself can be regarded as moving, curved space? There would seem to be room for doubt.

(c) Against the remaining Lokāyata position, that mind is a quality of the body, none of our authors offers any arguments—which is a pity, since it appears the most similar to modern materialist positions. In fact, an example given by Losang Gyatso even suggests this possibility. He says (p. 88) that no part of the body can pass into the nature of mind, just as sandalwood cannot become the nature of the smell of sandalwood. Since the smell of sandalwood is a quality of sandalwood, if the example were exact, then mind would be a quality of part of the body!

With Gyel-tsap Je,[81] the Lokāyatas' example is not the taste of beer but its potential to intoxicate, and Candrakīrti too gives a similar example:

> Just as from certain transformations on meeting some alcoholic products, is produced an intoxicating potential, which is a cause of intoxication and insensibility of living beings, so from a certain maturation of the material elements of the small oval embryo etc., minds are produced; and these come to distinguish all things.[82]

Candrakīrti, writing from the Prāsaṅgika viewpoint, does not refute this directly but argues that the Lokāyatas' views on other existences are unreliable since their perception even of this one is distorted; for they attribute true existence to the elements.

5 Buddhism, Science and Scientism

In contrast to the ancient Indian situation, materialism is now the accepted orthodoxy, and none of us can escape its influence. On all sides it is taken for granted that Science has disproved the concept of mind and everything "supernatural." Constantly, we hear religion dismissed as mere wishful thinking, unworthy of rational men, and explained away as compensation for class oppression, repressed sexuality, a childish longing for an all-powerful father, or whatever.

> Impotence of the exploited classes in their struggle against the exploiters just as inevitably gives rise to the belief in a better life after death as impotence of the savage in his battle with nature gives rise to belief in gods, devils, miracles, and the like....Religion is opium for the people. Religion is a sort of spiritual booze, in which the slaves of capital drown their human image, their demand for a life more or less worthy of man.[83]

Thus Lenin, who does not omit to promise in the same essay, "We shall always preach the scientific world outlook." This is an instance of *scientism*: a system of thought that claims to be scientific when in fact it is dogmatic and thus by nature unscientific.

If scientistic ideologues can appeal to science to justify their materialist views, it is only because materialism is firmly entrenched within science itself. For over a century, especially since the publication of Darwin's *The Origin of Species* in 1859, biologists have been telling us that we are no more than very complicated machines, who have come into existence by a series of chance processes. We are here only because our ancestors were more successful than others in the ruthless struggle for existence. There is no purpose to life except to compete and survive—any inclination to help other human beings is merely part of a hereditary behaviour pattern which happened to favour the survival of our species. *Mechanism*, the belief "that all living things are completely explicable in terms of the laws of physics and chemistry,"[84] has scored success after success, while the opposite approach of *vitalism*, the belief "that there is something distinctive about living matter which places it in a class above the level of the mere machine, no matter how complex the machine may be",[84] has been refuted on point after point and for most of this century has been virtually obsolete.

In face of this challenge to the Dharma, what can Buddhists do? Three main approaches are possible:

1.   *Fundamentalism*: maintain all the traditional beliefs of Tibetan Buddhists and reject Science entirely. This is Losang Gyatso's approach when he tries to laugh off the ideas that human beings evolved from lower animals and that perception of pain in the foot proceeds via transmission of a nervous impulse to the brain. It may be possible for Tibetans in India, but for us in the West it is not a live option.

2.   *Retreat*: define separate spheres of interest for Science and religion, accepting that physical truth must be mechanistic and leaving it to the scientists, while religion must be confined to spiritual truth. This approach has been adopted by many Christians, and perhaps one could prune the Buddhadharma so as not to trespass on the scientific domain.

3. *Synthesis*: recognising that mechanism and the Dharma cannot both be right, but that scientific observational evidence cannot be dismissed although its interpretation is subject to error, analyse Science critically in the light of the Dharma and arrive at a synthesis. In the process, certain elements of traditional Buddhist teachings will have to be eliminated as incompatible with observation—the teaching that the earth, sun and moon are flat disks is only the most obvious example. But if Buddhism is to become really effective in the West, this critique of Science is indispensable. As the evidence for rebirth listed in Chapter Three shows, it cannot fail to establish that the Dharma is far more reasonable than many people believe.

Science and the Dharma cannot fundamentally be opposed. Many in fact have been attracted to Buddhism through seeing it as in some sense scientific. Despite its imperfections and temporary aberrations, Science is in the long run an exceedingly powerful method of transcending the limitations of an individual human being and arriving at solidly-established truth. Its essence is honesty and a willingness to submit ideas to the test of observation and fair criticism. Nevertheless, at any particular time, some of the ideas current among scientists are inevitably erroneous and to be rejected in the end. The materialism which since Darwin has increasingly dominated biology is one such idea.

Darwin's contribution was twofold. First, he established clearly the fact of the evolution of species of animals and plants. This has been borne out by countless observations, in particular the beautiful demonstration of its genetic basis by molecular biology. It is the central unifying idea of biology, bringing order into the amazing diversity and complexity of the living world. Second, he presented a theory, explaining evolution in terms of the mechanical operation of blind chance, and this is another matter. While there certainly occurs adaptation of organisms to the environment by a process of natural selection similar to that which Darwin proposed,[85] it cannot be claimed that all biological evolution has been satisfactorily explained in this way. The facts are quite consistent with the concept of evolution as an intelligent process. But it is one thing to assert this and quite another to work out such a concept as a testable theory. For the present, Darwinian theory remains at the centre of biology, exerting its influence against religious ideas. (See for example the diatribe against religious systems of ethics that concludes Monod's important book *Chance and Necessity*.[86]) A scientist-mystic has described it as "a sinister force—perhaps the most sinister—that seriously threatens the ultimate good of the human soul."[87]

The non-mechanist critique of mechanistic biology probes three open wounds in its flesh: (1) the direct evidence for mind from parapsychology and rebirth memories; (2) the major unsolved problems and difficulties in evolutionary theory; and (3) modern physics. Angry reactions result, respectively (1) either a bland denial that there is any such evidence (totally untrue), or the claim that it is all faked, (2) pointing to earlier problems which eventually found mechanistic solutions and attacking the critic's motivation, accusing him of looking for a "God of the gaps" to prop up his doomed and discredited religion for a few last months, and (3) bitter attacks on physicists for a "loss of scientific confidence," "faltering" in respect of certainty, causality and rationality,[88] and poking their noses into biology where they do not belong.

The scientific evidence for parapsychological phenomena—telepathy, clairvoyance, precognition, and psychokinesis, in human beings and animals—despite confident assertions to the contrary, is now overwhelming. It can be countered only by supposing a vast conspiracy involving hundreds of people all over the world. Randall's account of the subject[89] is warmly recommended.

There is much discussion of the difficulties with neo-Darwinian theory by biologists themselves, of which any Buddhist who wishes to criticise Darwinism without making a fool of himself should take the trouble to become informed. A brief introduction is given in Randall's book, where further references may be found.

The foundation of biology is necessarily physics. But while biologists in general have yet to move into the post-mechanist age, the discovery of Relativity and Quantum Mechanics freed physicists from the crudely mechanical ways of thinking prevalent in the nineteenth century. As Merrell-Wolff[90] points out, "since 1896 physics has laid the foundation for mysticism with a vengeance," and it provides no support for the materialistic interpretation of Darwinism. Convincing evidence of the similarity of the physicist's and the mystic's world-views is given by LeShan,[91] who presents many quotations from the writings of physicists and mystics and invites the reader to judge which is which. Physics has abandoned the concept of things existing absolutely, from their own side, and recognises that phenomena depend very much on the observer and what observations he makes. All the information a physicist has comes through his sensory consciousnesses, thus he cannot avoid being concerned with mind in the end. So weird are the ideas of the physics of elementary particles that it is not too surprising to find a theoretical physicist elaborating a theory that electrons carry mind.[92] (However, this approach will obviously not be able to account for memories of past lives in a single chain, unmixed with other individuals, as observed, so like most of the ideas of theoretical physicists it will presumably be a dead end.)

Now, "There is but one indefectibly certain truth, and that is the truth that pyrrhonistic scepticism itself leaves standing—the truth that the present phenomenon of consciousness exists."[93] How then is it possible that the concept of mind as something more than the physical and chemical behaviour of the nervous system could have been eliminated from biology, to the extent that a neurobiologist can accuse those who are trying to reassert it of mounting "an attack, not merely against neurobiology but against the whole rational structure of science itself"?[94]

Hatred and fear of religion and mystery has played its part, but probably more important is our habit of rendering the world objective by stepping back into the role of an onlooker who does not belong to it. The physicist Schrödinger,[95] one of the builders of Quantum Mechanics, has explained clearly the errors that result. My mind constructs the objective, "real world" out of my sensations, perceptions and memories. Now this objective world includes both my own body and those of other people, which there is every reason to believe are linked with consciousness just as mine is. Thus I regard other people's minds as forming part of the real world around me, and because of the symmetry between others and myself I conclude that my own mind too forms part of the real world it constructed. I feel sure my conscious personality is inside my head, looking out from behind my eyes. Therefore I expect to find in the real world sensations of colours and sounds etc., and places where mind and matter interact. But since in fact my mind was never part of that world, and nor were others' minds, to which I have absolutely no direct subjective access, it follows that however hard I look I cannot find these sensations or interactions, but only matter behaving in exact accordance with the laws of physics and chemistry—pulses shooting along nerve fibres, transmitter substances diffusing across synapses to trigger other neurons and being mopped up by enzymes, and all the other intricate processes of the nervous system. Nowhere is there any objective evidence of the existence of mind or its interactions with matter. As Spinoza said, "Neither can the body determine the mind to think, nor the mind determine the body to motion or rest or anything else (if such there be)."[96] And yet, we seem to be responsible for our own deeds! Schrödinger considers this a paradox which can probably be overcome only by recognising that subject and object are one, but for practical purposes, in everyday life and scientific research, we have to discriminate subject and object. His system is thus comparable to the Buddhist Mind-Only system (*Citta-mātra*), with a similar presentation of the two levels of truth; however, he avoids speculating on the causes of sensory perceptions.

Thus it is quite in order that scientists should make the conscious decision to confine their studies to the objective world, to avoid extreme conceptual difficulties; in which case, in relation to that science, mind does not exist. It is also to be expected that some, not fully understanding the above reasoning, will draw exaggerated conclusions from the lack of objective evidence of mind-matter interactions. Monod, for example, claims: "Objective analysis obliges us to see that this seeming duality [of brain & spirit] within us is an illusion,"[97] evidently not realising that the question is beyond the scope of objective analysis.

It is interesting to note that another scientist, Franklin Merrell-Wolff, was led by meditative realisations to adopt a thoroughly Cittamātrin view-point. Making the important point,

> There seems to be but one fact of experience that affords the explanation of this attribution of reality-value to the material of physical science and that is that this material is relatively common and constant with respect to the vast majority of observers, and that so far as is

commonly known, no individual can success-
fully act as though this material were not,

he explains the "objective somewhat" as "a collective
phantasy projected from the collective unconscious."[98]

Now if karma produces a physical result, this would
seem to be an instance of mind-matter interaction. It
follows from Schrödinger's argument that looked at objectively, the result must follow ordinary scientific laws.
To take an example, a man is walking through a forest
when a heavy branch falls, killing him.[99] The scientific
explanation that the branch had been gradually wea-
kened by being eaten by insects to the point where it
could no longer support its own weight, and therefore
had to fall, is quite true. We are taught to be content with
this answer, and accept that the man's being underneath
just at that moment is merely a "coincidence." People
brought up differently look for a different sort of explanation, one that we would term "magical." Some would say
the man was killed by the branch because of sorcery by
an enemy, while a Tibetan lama would say it was the
man's karma. This karma, of course, does not exist objectively, at least in relation to ordinary beings, so it is
useless as a scientific explanation. But supposing that the
man's consciousness did indeed (subjectively, for him)
carry a karmic imprint tending to attract such a death, we
see that there is no conflict between the scientific and
karmic explanations, and the mind-matter interaction
shows up in the objective world as a coincidence.

Likewise at conception, according to Science, the egg
carries half the mother's genes, selected at random within
each gene-pair, and each of the spermatozoa carries a
different selection of about half the father's genes, and
the egg could have been fertilised by any one of thousands of spermatozoa, so the resulting genetic constitu-
tion of the baby is determined by chance. As long as

suitable genes exist in the parents—which does not necessarily mean either parent must display these characteristics—it may be clever or stupid, dark or fair, male or female, oval-faced or square-faced, etc. But for the Buddhist, these characteristics are determined by the karma carried by the baby's continuum from its previous lives. Though this causal chain from the baby's previous existences seems to cut right across the genetic one from the parents, it is important to understand that there is no incompatibility at all. Both the genetic explanation of the baby's characteristics and the karmic explanation must be simultaneously true. Just as in the first example, what appears to be mere chance in the objective world, the choice of genes, is a mind-matter interaction in the Buddhist account. This point is stressed since the misconception is frequent that if karma is true, genetics must be wrong. This is doubtless aided by the gross misunderstandings of genetics prevalent among Buddhist writers.[100] But if the two explanations really were contradictory, it is the karmic one we would have to discard, for the validity of genetics is strongly established by many years of observation. Genetics is the physical aspect of the means through which karma operates to produce the ripe karmic result (*vipāka-phala*).

Other supposed instances of mind-matter interactions, such as parapsychological phenomena, also manifest objectively as events in accordance with the laws of physical science but classed as "coincidences."[101] If a clairvoyant such as Edgar Cayce describes the exact movements of a man half a continent away, no-one doubts his speech is produced in the normal way through signals from his brain operating the relevant muscles, likewise the man's movements: what is special is the "coincidence" that they match.

Equally, Monod[102] tells us that evolution is determined by mutations which, by the laws of Quantum Mechanics, and by the coincidental nature of their functional effects, are purely chance events. Who can say that mind is not participating here also?

Since genetics and karma cannot conflict, it follows there is no reason for Buddhists to object to the idea of the genetic inheritance of certain mental qualities such as intelligence. That differences of intelligence are subjectively real is confirmed by people's recall of having been more or less intelligent in previous lives. Considering how stupid most animals are compared with most humans, it can hardly be claimed that physical characteristics cannot influence mental capabilities. Clearly one's genetic potential for intelligence is part of the ripe karmic result.

However, it is possible for an explanation in terms of karma to be erroneous and open to disproof. A verse by Āryaśūra (*Jātaka-mālā* xxix.12) says:

> Though he be lacking clear power of the mind,
> And his faculties be of foolish nature,
> Any newborn babe, without instruction,
> Makes endeavours in the eating of food
> And makes endeavours to drink milk at the
>   breast.
> This is through habit in other, previous lives.
>   (LG, p. 66)

Such instinctive activities as an infant's seeking the breast, seeking, eating and digesting food, excretion, and breathing are all adduced as evidence for previous existences (LG 56–66), on the ground that they would be inexplicable but for habits of the same activities from previous lives. That is, they are asserted to be result similar to the cause (*niṣyanda-phala*) and not genetically determined (*vipāka-phala*). But if instinctive behaviours were not inherited from the parents, it would follow that different individuals of the same species would have quite different instinctive behaviours, corresponding to their different previous existences; whereas in fact, animals, especially insects, are often observed to have very complicated instinctive behaviours, shown by all individuals of the particular species and distinct from the behaviour of other species. Ways of breathing, digesting food, & so on, also differ from species to species. The facts are consistent with genetic inheritance of these behaviour patterns and inconsistent with the "habit" explanation. That a mechanistic explanation of breathing etc. in terms of inheritance is adequate can be seen by reflecting that one could construct a machine that would perform any of these activities, without any possibility of "previous habits."

From Schrödinger's argument, we can also see why karma in general is so profound and hard to understand. To understand the interaction process and its physical aspect involves understanding both the ultimate and conventional truths, from the Cittamātrin viewpoint; and to understand these simultaneously is something only a Buddha can do. Even if less than full realisation is sufficient, it is still likely to be difficult.

6 *Details of Rebirth*

Establishing the mere fact of rebirth by no means establishes the whole Buddhist doctrine of rebirth. Points of the doctrine that are important for the meditations on the Stages of the Path are: (1) One is not necessarily reborn as a human being, but in any of a limitless variety of states of existence, most of them invisible to us. (2) When human beings die, it is most unlikely that their next rebirths will be human unless they have been exceptionally virtuous. Almost certainly they will be reborn in a lower state, with great suffering, and remain in such states for eons before gaining another human existence, which is the only state with an appreciable chance of practising the Dharma. (3) One's past lives have no beginning. One has experienced every possible samsaric state infinite times and been in every possible relationship with every other sentient being. Also (4) one passes from one life to the next via an intermediate state. Let us examine these points in the light of the evidence now available.

1. *Non-human rebirths*

While there are limitless possible states of rebirth corresponding to the limitless variety of karmas of sentient beings, they are classified into five or six major realms, according to which emotion predominates, as Milarepa explains:

> Great hatred is the fetter of hell,
> Great avarice the *preta*'s chain,
> Great delusion the animal's.
> Great desire is the human fetter,
> Great jealousy is the *asura*'s,
> And great pride the *deva*'s chain.
> These are six fetters binding one from Free-
> dom.[103]

In the fivefold classification, *devas* and *asuras* are counted as one realm.

I find only one report of a *deva* existence in the modern literature. Story[104] tells of an Indian man who claimed that towards the end of a life as a butcher in China, he had given up killing animals and eating meat, and in consequence was then born as a *deva*. After a long time in the *deva* realm, he took his present rebirth. The only detail of the *deva* realm reported is that the *devas* dressed in Chinese style.

The animal realm is the only non-human realm whose inhabitants are generally visible to humans. One of Story's[105] subjects, a Buddhist born in Burma, was convinced he had been a horse in his previous life. His meditation was constantly disturbed by a jingling like harness bells, "a sensation of moving along, and from time to time prickling and tickling sensations...in various parts of his body, as though he were being bitten by flies." When he sought to brush them off, he would find there were no flies in the room. Hypnotic regression produced the same sensations. He looked rather horse-like, his voice had a horselike quality, and he had rather a slow mind and a knack of getting on with horses.

In principle, verification of a horse rebirth is possible. A traditional Cathar story[106] tells of a man who recollects having been a horse and losing his shoe in a particular place, of which he tells his companion. Then a search is made in the indicated spot and the horseshoe found.

The subject of Pisani's book,[107] also, in the middle of a long series of human existences going back more than eleven thousand years, recalled a life as a lioness. He did not feel this existence was inferior to the human, nor that he was condemned to it as a result of unskilful actions, but that he chose it as a valuable experience in order to gain understanding.

The same subject also remembered having been a tree.[108] Buddhist doctrine denies the possibility of rebirth as a plant, but admits that there can be spirit beings whose consciousness is karmically bound to a tree or even to a mountain (LG 20).

There is one clear case of a *preta* existence, i.e. a spirit existence dominated by craving: the Karen house-boy examined by Francis Story.[109] He had an unusual congenital malformation of the hands and feet—deep linear indentations, the right hand being underdeveloped past the line across the palm, and three toes joined at birth. Sometimes his right arm would swell and he would feel severe pain in all the affected parts. He remembered having been the son of a rich man, who left him three houses and much silver and other treasure. After his father's death he lived alone, without servants, in one of the houses. One night robbers broke in, bound him tightly with wire with his hands between his legs, and made off with all his silver and jewellery. He spent three days dying in agony, with blood dripping from the cuts in his hands and congealing between three of his toes. Then he found himself looking at his body; then he wandered about for a long time, "his whole existence in a single idea which was like an obsession: the loss of his wealth and the desire to recover it." Finally he became aware of living beings, was attracted to a certain young woman, and was reborn as her child.

While many observations of spirit beings have been reported by people with psychic powers, it should not be assumed that all these are *pretas*. They can include *devas*, beings in the intermediate state, and even hell-beings. "Ghosts" may not be present living persons at all; according to Joan Grant,[35] a ghost is a split-off fragment of a personality, with a limited energy which eventually runs down.

The recollections of hells I have found reported are limited to the far memory experts. Elisabeth Haich[42] describes unforgettably how she broke the ancient Egyptian equivalent of a Tantric root vow and fell into a special kind of hell state, bound immovably to her mummified body for 3000 years, during which there was nothing by which to judge the passage of time, so it seemed infinite:

> The feeling of horror and fear refuses to leave me for a single moment.... I cannot look in any direction for help for my tortured soul.... The tortures and sufferings know no end...no end...no end....[110]

She then lived many lives as a woman before at last, in her present life, she regained the realisations she had lost. In Buddhist terminology this would be a *pratyeka-naraka*, an individual hell.

Joan Grant[111] has described a "visit" to the Caverns of the Underworld, which was part of her initiation in Ist Dynasty Egypt. There, "people expiate those crimes which are too manifold to be freed on Earth." A former Peruvian priest who had slain thousands in human sacrifice feels his heart being torn out again and again, his torturer being but a vision of himself. A woman "whose presence in a house had always disturbed the quiet of them who shared it with her, until it was as though their rest was tormented with stinging insects," is beset by hornets. People who had maltreated animals are now themselves in tortured animal bodies, such as a monkey with its paws cut off.

The same author has also reported an individual hell, in Crete, where a former sorcerer, who had forced some young girls to eat filth for magical purposes until one rebelled and poisoned him, has been imprisoned for 500 years eating filth himself and reliving his death agony. "Caught in an eternal now, he knows only the present, and to him this endless horror is for ever fresh."[112] A case she encountered in this life,[35] of a man who had committed suicide by jumping from the fifth floor of the Palace Hotel, Brussels, five days before she was given his room, and was still continuously repeating the leap in a state of panic fear, is comparable except for the time scale.

Apart from such a recent case, where the fact of the suicide was readily confirmed, there can of course be no verification of these reports. Their value depends entirely on the degree of confidence one places in their authors. Joan Grant's books are far too beautiful to be really false, and are quite consistent with Buddhist teachings translated from the symbolic and not literally credible forms of the scriptures into examples which are psychologically realistic. Haich's book, too, despite certain difficulties with the esoteric teachings she recounts, conveys a powerful impression of the meaning of renunciation and Bodhicitta, and the dangers involved in Tantra-like practices.

2. *Rarity of the human rebirth*

That one unconvincing *deva*, two animal, one tree, one *preta* and one hell existences have been recalled as against several thousand human existences appears difficult to reconcile with the Buddhist teachings that human existences are extremely rare. However, there are good reasons why one would not expect to have records of many existences in the realms of woe even if they do exist.

In the case of Edgar Cayce's life readings, the hypnotic

suggestion employed called for "appearances on the earth plane...in each life which built or retarded the entity's development."[113] This effectively excluded non-human lives, so it is not surprising that Cayce refers to non-human states only indirectly—he attributes some cases of mental disease to possession by discarnate entities.[114] It is entirely reasonable that lives with the most karmic influence on this human life would also be human.

In most of the hypnotic regression experiments, certainly in Wambach's, precautions are taken to stop the subject experiencing anything too distressing. There is therefore no possibility of recalling a hell existence even if this were consistent with the other suggestions given. In any case, experiences of extreme suffering are resistant to recall. Nevertheless, the sparsity of animal rebirths recalled is still difficult to account for if we have been born animal more often than human in the last few millennia, as the teachings assert.

There are many examples of people experiencing long series of human lives with not more than a few centuries between each, and sometimes much less. Above all, Wambach's experiment[57] showed that at each of the time periods checked between 2000 BC and 500 AD, roughly seven percent of the sample of present-day Americans remembered being alive. From 1000 AD to the present century, the proportion increased sharply. This implies that virtually the whole human population in the historical past is accounted for by past lives of human beings now living.[115] Also, the great majority of Wambach's subjects remembered past human lives. Therefore there is strong evidence that the human race consists of a group of individuals repeatedly taking human rebirth, with a very little interchange with other large mammals.

It seems then that in the short term—say a dozen existences—the picture of our rebirth prospects presented in the Buddhist teachings is exaggeratedly black. But this does not mean we can afford to be complacent. Firstly, the commonness of human rebirth at the present is altogether exceptional. Human beings have only been present on Earth at all for a tiny fraction of the history of life here, and the unprecedentedly high population of the moment cannot be expected to continue. In a few years, human existence could be much rarer and more difficult to obtain. Secondly, our data are very crude and limited and it could well be that on a slightly longer timescale there is a large chance of degenerating to an animal state without hope of quick recovery. Thirdly, the standards of behaviour required of one are not absolute but depend on what one is capable of: an action which would be negligeable in an ordinary person can indeed mean hell for an advanced Dharma practitioner, as Haich's example shows.

We could probably learn more about the nature and commonness of our non-human existences by hypnotic regression experiments designed specifically to investigate them. There seems to be no reason why Buddhists themselves should not undertake such research.

3. *Beginningless mind*

Losang Gyatso (p. 109) argues:

> Just establishing that a previous homogeneous continuum must precede establishes that rebirths are beginningless. For what is not a sentient being cannot be made into a sentient being, and non-mind cannot be made into mind. As, for example, before that hen came an egg; and before that egg came another hen; so there is no initial limit one can reach.

The example illustrates perfectly both the strength and the limitations of the argument. We know[116] that if one goes back enough generations, the ancestors of that hen were less and less hen-like, passing through various kinds of birds to *Archaeopteryx* (part reptile, part bird) some 150 million years ago, and before that, reptilian ancestors. These descended from amphibians, who descended from fish, who probably descended from worm-like creatures, whose ancestors as one goes still farther back must have been more and more primitive. This description of the descent of the hen from fish is deduced from the very assumption that any animal is born from parents which are similar to it, together with careful examination of living and fossil animals.

Few would deny that the ancient fish and the modern hen were different "types," yet they are linked by a direct line of descent in which each animal is no more unlike its parents than we are unlike ours. Over 300 or 400 million years, trivial differences between parents and children add up to the difference between a fish and a hen. Applying Postulate P1 in the strict form assumed by Losang Gyatso, the ancestors of the hen 400 million years ago would still have had to be hens. Thus the theory based on repeated application of the postulate breaks down in practice, since types are not absolute but merge gradually into each other.

When one extrapolates from the known to the unknown, the farther one extrapolates, the more likely one is to be wrong; and if one extrapolates to infinity, as in the prediction that my personal continuum as an individual sentient being is infinitely old, one is almost certain to be wrong. Within the theory, it is a logical deduction; but to assert that it is actually true is the wildest speculation.

Not only is there continuity between fish and hens: there is continuity between plants and animals, since there exist single-celled organisms such as *Chlamydomonas*, *Euglena*, *Polytoma* and *Volvox* which have characteristics of both, and have been classified by zoologists as Protozoa (in the animal kingdom) and by botanists with the algae (in the plant kingdom).[117] Multicelled plants and animals too are seen to be intimately related when one examines the structure and chemistry of their individual cells. These facts are hard to explain unless both plants and animals evolved from common ancestors. Thus since plants, by Buddhist doctrine, are non-sentient, while at least the higher animals are sentient, biology reveals continuity between sentient and non-sentient organisms. This at least suggests that the distinction between sentient and non-sentient may not be absolute. Thus just as hens are beginningless in that one cannot point to a first hen, but still there have not always been hens, so my mind doubtless lacks a beginning one can point to, but still this does not necessarily mean it has existed infinitely long.

The view that my mind is infinitely old is an extreme which leads to difficulties, like any view of self-existence. Indeed, it is among the fourteen theories to which the Buddha many times refused to assent, "that the world is eternal, or not, or both, or neither; or finite, or infinite, or both, or neither...," condemning them as "the jungle of theorising, the wilderness of theorising, the tangle of theorising, the bondage and shackles of theorising, attended by ill, distress, perturbation and fever, conducing not to detachment, passionlessness, tranquillity, peace, to knowledge and wisdom of *Nirvāṇa*."[118] We can easily show how it leads to distress.

The *Lam rim* proponents assert that I have been circling in *saṃsāra* infinitely long, passing through every samsaric state infinite times, and undergoing every possible relationship with every other sentient being infinite times. If it is possible to attain liberation from *saṃsāra* by following the Path, there must be a point P on the Path which is the first point at which it is certain one will attain Liberation within a finite time. Likewise there must be a point Q on the Path which is the first point at which it is certain one will not fall again into the lower realms. If Q precedes P, there will be a class of beings who have attained Q but not P and are thus circling forever in the upper samsaric realms without possibility of falling into lower realms. This is contrary to doctrine, therefore Q either coincides with, or is later than, P.

Consider now the point R on the Path, preceding P by one thought-moment. Since it precedes P, it follows a person at R must still expect to take infinitely long to reach Liberation. By the same objection as to Q preceding P, he can hardly spend this infinite waiting time poised at R but must fall again to circle in *saṃsāra* as before. R is thus an ordinary samsaric state through which I have already passed infinite times. Infinite times have I set out on the Path and traversed the first section to arrive at R; infinite times have I reached the impenetrable barrier which divides R from P, and infinite times been turned back to cycle for further endless ages in the six realms. If Buddhas have taught the means by which this frightful wall can be crossed, I have heard it from their lips times beyond number, and it availed me naught. Already I have tried everything—how can I hope for Liberation this time? If I enter the Path yet again, my chance of following it beyond R is exactly zero.

We note also that since each moment there are beings attaining Perfect Enlightenment, infinite beings must already have done so, therefore if each sentient being has always existed, the number of sentient beings must also be infinite. In this case it does not necessarily follow that every one of them has been my mother even if I have been born from a womb or an egg infinite times— mathematically it is perfectly possible that only an infinitesimal fraction have. It is not without reason that Venerable Geshe Rabten frequently mentions[119] it is extremely difficult to persuade oneself that all sentient beings have been one's mother, and recommends Śāntideva's method of developing *Bodhicitta*, which avoids the fearsome difficulties of these infinities.

One does not have to read many Buddhist texts to become aware of the arbitrariness of the insanely large numbers frequently quoted and the lack of mathematical sophistication of the Buddhist pandits. It seems unlikely they really understood how unbridgeable is the gulf between the finite and the infinite. We can take their "infinities" non-literally when necessary. They are meant to impress on us that we have endured far more existences than we care to think, but surely not to take away all hope of Liberation.

4. The Intermediate State

The intermediate state is contemplated in Lam-rim meditations on the mechanism of samsara, as a more straightforward alternative to the twelve links of Dependent Arising (*pratītya-samutpāda*), and is of natural interest since we all have to pass through it.

The majority of earlier Buddhist schools, including the Mahāsaṅghikas and their branches, the Ekavyāvahārikas and Kukkuṭikas, and the Vibhajya-vādins, Mahīśāsakas, Dharmaguptakas and Theravādins, denied that there was an intermediate existence (*antarābhava*) between death and rebirth.[120-1] The Theravādin text *Visuddhimagga*,[122] and texts by Nāgārjuna[123] and Candrakīrti,[124] teach that the aggregates of the rebirth existence re-emerge immediately, without a gap, in dependence on those of the dying existence when these cease. Nothing whatsoever passes from one existence to the next—it is like one lamp being lit from the flame of another. The *Mahāprajñāpāramitā-śāstra*,[125] attributed to Nāgārjuna, also asserts, in refutation of a claim that a subtle body continues after death to form the body in the intermediate existence, that the aggregates of the intermediate existence are abandoned at the same moment as they are taken up.

However, the Sammatīyas, Sarvāstivādins, Sautrāntikas, Pūrvaśailas (a later Mahāsaṅghika school) and later Mahīśāsakas maintained there was an intermediate existence.[120] Vasubandhu gives an extensive account in the commentary to *Abhidharma-kośa*,[126] and Asaṅga continued this tradition, in *Abhidharma-samuccaya*[127] and the *Yogācāra-bhūmi*. Tsongkhapa's account in the *Lam rim chen mo*[128] is based on these three works. Several sutras support them, which their opponents can explain away only by altering the text or by nonsensical interpretations. For example, three conditions necessary for conception are taught: union of the parents, fertility of the mother, and the presence of a "Gandharva," i.e. a being in the intermediate state. The Theravādins distort this into a superstitious and essentially unBuddhist theory by interpreting the Gandharva as a sort of deity "said to preside over child-conception."[129]

Vasubandhu describes the intermediate being thus[130]:

Because it has the same thrower, it has
The form of the coming living existence,
That is, th' existence before [the next] death
And later than the moment of birth.

It is seen by its peers, with the pure divine eye,
And is karmically possessed of magical powers.
Its faculties are complete, it's unobstructed,
Can't be diverted, and feeds on smells.

One whose mind is perverted goes
To his place of migration through lustfulness.
Others, desiring a smell or abode.
The hell being, with his feet above.

The intermediate existence is a preliminary to the coming birth, which has already been karmically "thrown" at the moment of death. An intermediate being to be reborn as human will have the form of a child of five or six, naked, and with perfect faculties, including either male or female sex. It can go anywhere instantly, unobstructed by matter. Karmically endowed with the divine eye, it sees, even a long way away, its place of birth and its future parents copulating. If it is male, it feels sexual desire for the mother and hostility to the father; if female, inversely. Joining them and imagining itself to be making love with the parent of opposite sex, it finds itself "born" in the womb. Beings to be born "from heat and moisture," such as insects, are attracted by smells, and those to be born miraculously by desire for an abode—for example, a being to be born in the hot hells is tormented by the cold wind and rain and wants somewhere warm.[131]

According to Tsongkhapa, the vision of the parents copulating is illusory, but once the sexual desire has arisen the being cannot avoid taking birth there, all it can see is the genitals thrashing about and this makes it angry, whereupon it takes birth. Apparently it is necessary for both emotions, desire and anger, to arise. There is disagreement on the duration of the intermediate existence, but the Tibetans have settled on a maximum of seven weeks, with a change of body after each week.

We now have considerable observational evidence with which to compare the pandits' assertions, from the sources described in Chapter Three. It is harder to remember the experience of birth and before birth than to remember previous lives—just under half of Wambach's subjects were able to do so under hypnosis, as against ninety percent[132] or ninety-five percent[133] remembering previous lives, and Mme Desjardins[47] quotes a similar figure. Even so, Wambach amassed 750 people's reports of these experiences.[59]

Story[134] sums up the spontaneous recollections of the intermediate existence:

These memories show an underlying unity of pattern.... At first the disembodied entity is not aware that death has taken place. The sensations described resemble those of persons who have had experiences of the disembodied consciousness under anaesthesia or in what is known as astral projection.... A feature which frequently occurs in these memories is the appearance of a guide who assists and directs the discarnate entity.

Story's data confirm some of the assertions. Certainly the intermediate state exists with its own characteristics not belonging to the five destinies. The intermediate being does indeed have clear faculties and powers of unobstructed movement, and can see other spirits. Private Keaw of Thailand, for example, having died of cholera, watched monks performing a ceremony at his house, then as they were leaving, he:

> noticed certain peculiarities about his own body and realised for the first time that he was dead. He then followed the monks. Everything seemed ordinary to him except that he was able to walk through people and as soon as he thought of a place he immediately found himself there. He did not feel hungry....he was afraid of a drunken man walking and of a child in case they should fall on him. Keaw seemingly felt himself to be very small. He could not remember being angry but had seen other spirits angry at living persons who threw stones or spat. They feared they might be hit.[135]

Tsongkhapa's assertion, after the *Yogācāra-bhūmi*, that no desire for the previous body arises, is also abundantly confirmed from all sources. But other assertions fare less well. Some sources indicate that the intermediate being does not immediately take on the form of his next existence as a naked child, but at first is clothed as at the time of death. Indeed, when recently deceased persons appear to relatives, they are seen in their previous form and wearing the clothes they had on when they died. In fact, it seems that what the next birth is to be is usually chosen in the intermediate existence, in discussion with others, although within what limits is not yet clear. Most of Wambach's sample remembered such discussions, the counsellors often being relatives and friends, with no distinction between people alive or dead at the time of decision. Fifty-nine percent had more than one counsellor. In Story's cases, the guide was often an old man, the "yogi in white," or an old woman.

It is common for deceased persons to attend their own funeral ceremonies, as in the case quoted above. Many continue for a while to observe their loved ones and relatives, as did Bridey Murphy. The intermediate existence generally seems to be free of suffering compared with earthly life, without the physical pain, hunger and fatigue of the gross body, but can feel empty and with limited power of action and communication. There is a kind of timelessness in it, a detachment from earth time so that decades or more can just drift by. There is not the slightest evidence of a seven-week lifetime with a change of body after each week. On the contrary, many of Wambach's subjects felt they had chosen the late twentieth century to experience a lifetime for some particular reason (more than seventy percent mentioning that this time would be characterised by a new development of spiritual awareness). Vasubandhu's view[136] that the intermediate existence lasts as long as it takes for the conditions for the required birth to come together, although dismissed by Tsongkhapa as lacking reputable authority,[137] seems more realistic.

As to the manner of taking birth, alas for the Buddhist theory which so delighted Freudians, no-one reports having seen the parents making love and desired one and hated the other. Some of Story's spontaneous cases felt an attraction to the mother and followed her about, one entered some water she was drinking, one embraced her round the neck, all seem to have lost consciousness (in accordance with *Abhidharmakośa* III.16); none mentions the father. Two-thirds of Wambach's subjects were reluctant to be born but accepted it as a disagreeable necessity. This compares with ninety percent who found death was pleasant. Human rebirth is not a simple matter of grabbing a body at all costs so that one can enjoy sensual pleasures. Many of us come here to learn and develop. Wambach asked her subjects the purpose of their present lifetime, and classified the answers as follows: twenty-five percent to gain additional experience, eighteen percent to work out their relationships with people known in past lives, eighteen percent to learn to give love, twenty-seven percent to grow spiritually and to teach others, and twelve percent other.[138]

Edgar Cayce's readings assert many times

> that the moment of conception does not coincide with the entrance of the soul. The readings frequently counsel expectant mothers to watch their thoughts during the period of pregnancy, inasmuch as the character of these thoughts to some degree determines the type of entity attracted to them.... The soul can enter the body shortly before birth, shortly after birth, or at the moment of birth. As much as twenty-four hours can elapse after an infant is born before the soul makes entry, and in some cases there are even last-minute changes with regard to the entity which will enter.[139]

This is in full agreement with the answers to Wambach's question, "When does your soul enter the foetus?" Thirty-three percent entered just before or during the birth process—two twins, for example, entered shortly before birth, fighting over which body to pick. Twenty percent were outside the foetus and nineteen percent in and out of the foetus during the period before birth, five percent were able to leave the foetus at will even after birth, twelve percent attached to it after six months' gestation, and only eleven percent were inside it in the first six months. She also found that eighty-six percent were aware of feelings, emotions and thoughts of the mother before they were born.[140] Story[141] too reports a striking case of a Thai man who became the child of his younger sister, born the day before he died. At his funeral, he remembered the birth and straight away was beside his sister and the baby. She twice told him he was dead and should go away, but he was strongly attracted, then lost consciousness and had a sensation of falling. Next he found he was a young baby. When he could talk, he retained considerable detailed knowledge from his previous life, such as the names of his former relatives, and the abilities to read Cambodian characters and to speak Laotian. These data cast grave doubt on the validity of models such as Losang Gyatso's, which insist that the very subtle body from the previous existence must be present for the foetus to develop. They show that the process of conception is not necessarily governed by the karma of the person to whom the body will belong.

To sum up the four points investigated here, it would appear that while some points of Buddhist teaching on rebirth are realistic, others are mythic or symbolic rather than literal, and others again are mere speculative elaborations that will have to be discarded when further investigation has given us a clearer picture of what actually happens. (1) There is some indication—scientific evidence would be hard to come by—that human beings can indeed be born in non-human states, either as animals or without gross physical form; but (2) runs of at least several human lifetimes in succession are the rule rather than the vanishingly rare exception, once one has attained the human state. (3) The doctrine that every sentient being's mental continuum is beginningless does not imply it has existed an infinite time, but an indefinite and doubtless excessively long time. Finally (4), it is established that we do experience an intermediate existence between human lives, in a subtle body which is not obstructed by gross matter and can travel anywhere as fast as thought. However, the standard Buddhist account of the manner of taking birth as a human being seems to be a myth teaching that samsaric rebirth is caused by desire and anger, rather than a description of what is actually experienced. In fact, birth apparently involves some sort of decision taken in consultation with others, often with a view to learning and spiritual development. We should be able to learn much more about the intermediate existence by careful research using hypnosis, and perhaps about our non-human existences also.

7 Conclusions

We have shown that it is important for a would-be
practitioner of the Dharma to understand that rebirth
exists, that it is nonsense to claim the Buddha did not
teach it, and that there is much evidence, some of it of a
high scientific standard, that it is a fact. Reviewing the
attempts to prove the existence of rebirth by Buddhist
scholastic logic, we found that some rested on superstitious beliefs disproved by modern observations, and
others on sweeping, dogmatic assumptions that must
appear doubtful to many and are denied by materialists.

Materialism is now very strong and by no means easy
to rebut. Modern materialism is founded on the mechanistic ideas of nineteenth-century Science, which although superseded in the most fundamental of sciences,
Physics, yet thrive at the heart of Biology and also linger
on in scientistic ideologies such as Marxism. It is urged
that Western Buddhists should neither ignore Science
nor beat a headlong retreat before it, but work towards a
new synthesis. In the past, whenever the Buddhadharma
has been newly introduced to a country, it has been
adapted by a judicious assimilation of indigenous traditions. In Tibet, for example, elements of the Bön religion
were absorbed and Bön in turn was transformed in
response to the Buddhist critique. It cannot be claimed
that the Dharma has been established in the West until it
is possible for anyone to accept Buddhist teachings without feeling that they conflict with scientific truth. At

present, any educated person in the West automatically rejects many traditional Buddhist teachings as superstition. All reject such doctrines as the flat Earth and spontaneous generation of insects, but many extend the rejection not only to all forms of ritual, monasticism, and deity practices, but also to the teachings on rebirth, and thus can accept most of Buddhist doctrine only in terms of weak, symbolic interpretations. It is therefore necessary that scientific method be absorbed into the Dharma, and Buddhist doctrines be submitted to scientific test where possible. While many picturesque theories will certainly have to be discarded or modified as a result, the Dharma can only gain in strength and universality by open-minded, impartial research—research which is neither credulous nor dogmatically sceptical.

We have seen that rebirth is a fact of experience, now open to scientific investigation. The beginnings of such investigation are sketched in Chapter Six, showing that we should not reject out of hand the possibility that we can be reborn in non-human states, even if it is less likely than traditionally taught, and that using hypnotic regression, we should be able to build up a more realistic picture of what we experience in the intermediate existence between human lives. Buddhists surely cannot neglect this technique, which promises to be so valuable not merely as a means of research into areas formerly accessible only to accomplished yogins, but as a direct aid to individual practice.

Whether Buddhists participate or not, scientific research into rebirth and such related areas as parapsychology, religious experience, out-of-the-body experiences and near-death experiences is bound to continue and grow into a body of religious science acceptable to people the world over, as Physics and Chemistry are today. It will certainly contribute to the great blossoming of spiritual awareness which is gradually gathering momentum. May this article too play its part in this awakening.

References and Notes

1 Desjardins, Arnaud: *Les Chemins de la Sagesse*, Tome III. Paris, La Table Ronde, 1972. p.22.
2 Conze, Edward: *Memoirs of a Modern Gnostic*, Vol.II. Sherborne, Samizdat Publishing Company, 1979. p.33.
3 *Lalitavistara*. Ed. P.L. Vaidya. Buddhist Skt. Texts, No.I. Darbhanga (Bihar), Mithila Inst., 1958. Ch.XXII, pp.250.13−19.
4 Ib., pp.250.24−251.7. cf. also Tib. transln: Tog Palace Kgr, *mDo sde, Kha.*
5 Tib. transln of *Vinaya-vastu*: Tog Palace Kgr, '*Dul ba, Nga*, 56.3−62.5.
6 *Vinaya-piṭaka* III.36, see transln by I.B. Horner in Conze (ed.): *Buddhist Texts through the Ages*. New York, Harper Torchbooks, 1964, pp.60−62.
7 *Sāmaññaphala-sutta: Dīgha-nikāya*, Sutta 2. In J.Block, J.Filliozat & L.Renou: *Canon Bouddhique Pāli (Tipiṭaka), Texte et Traduction. Sutta-piṭaka: Dīgha-nikāya.* Tome I, Fasc.I. Paris, Adrien-Maisonneuve, 1949. See pp.72−74.
8 Quoted by Nāgārjuna in *Sūtra-samuccaya*. Eng. transln: Bhikkhu Pāsādika, Linh-Son Publications d'Études Bouddhologiques, No.7, p.25.
9 Ib. No.7, p.26 to No.8, p.26.
10 *Laṅkāvatāra-Sūtra*, Chap.8 (Transln D.T. Suzuki, London, Routledge & Kegan Paul, 1932, p.220).
11 *Aṣṭasāhasrikā-prajñāpāramitā*, Ch.VII (Transln E.

Conze, Bolinas, Calif., Four Seasons Foundation, 1973. pp.139–141).

12   e.g. *Sāmaññaphala-sutta*, Ref.7.

13   Conze, E. (transl): *The Large Sutra on Perfect Wisdom*. Berkeley, Univ. Calif. Press, 1975. pp.66–74.

14   *The Middle Way*, most issues. For a particularly crass example, *48*, pp.66–70, 1973.

15   Dayal, Har: *The Bodhisattva Doctrine in Buddhist Sanskrit Literature*. Delhi, Motilal Banarsidass, 1970. p.73.

16   *Shorter Oxford English Dictionary*.

17   See Murti, T.R.V.: *The Central Philosophy of Buddhism*. London, Unwin Paperbacks, 1980, p.32; who, however, has not realised that "soul" does not necessarily imply a permanent substance.

18   *Kāśyapa-parivarta*, 64. Tog Palace Kgr, *dKon brtsegs, Cha*, 443.3, corrected after *Prasanna-padā* 248 (see Murti, Ref.17, p.164).

19   Head, Joseph, & S.L. Cranston (ed.): *Reincarnation: An East-West Anthology*. Wheaton, Illinois, Quest Book, 1968.

20   Conze, Ref.2, p.21.

21   Kant, Immanuel: *Prolegomena to Any Future Metaphysics*. Appendix. Transln in R.P. Wolff (ed.): *Ten Great Works of Philosophy*, New York, Mentor Books, 1969. p.392.

22   Wambach, Ref. 57, p.97, for example.

23   Story, Ref.29, p.213.

24   Ib., p.275 n.5. The data given by Wambach (Ref.57) also support this assertion.

25   Story, ib., p.185.

26   Ib., pp.201–2.

27   Figures from Alaux, Janine: *Et vous, où étiez-vous en 1673?* In *Marie Claire*, no.311, July 1978.

28   Stevenson, Ian: *Twenty Cases Suggestive of Reincarnation*. Univ. Press of Virginia, 2nd edition, 1974. Also numerous other publications.

29 Story, Francis: *Rebirth as Doctrine and Experience*: Essays and Case Studies. Kandy, Sri Lanka, Buddhist Publ. Soc., 1975.

29a Much valuable information on Rinpoches is to be found in Daniel Bärlocher's enthralling collection of interviews, *Testimonies of Tibetan Tulkus*, Rikon, Tibet-Institut, 1982.

30 *Mahāyāna-sūtrālaṃkāra*, XV, 11−14 (Tib. chapter numbering).

31 cf. *Vinaya-vastu*, Ref.5, p.57.3. *Mara* in the present context may be taken as an acronym for Machines, Aircraft, Radios & related devices, and Automobiles.

32 Ref.7, para.133.

33 Lilly, John C.: *The Centre of the Cyclone*. London, Paladin.

34 Lilly, John & Antonietta: *The Dyadic Cyclone*. London, Paladin, 1978.

35 Grant, Joan, & Denys Kelsey: *Many Lifetimes*. London, Victor Gollancz, 1968.

36 Grant, Joan: *Winged Pharaoh*. London, Arthur Barker, 1937; Sphere Books, 1973.

37 Grant, Joan: *Eyes of Horus*. London, Eyre Methuen, 1942; Corgi Books, 1975.

38 Grant, Joan: *Lord of the Horizon*. Eyre Methuen, 1944; Corgi, 1975.

39 Grant, Joan: *So Moses Was Born*. Eyre Methuen, 1952; Corgi, 1975.

40 Weatherhead, Leslie D.: *The Case for Reincarnation*. Tadworth (Surrey), M.C. Peto, 1958.

41 See Pisani, Ref.52.

42 Haich, Elisabeth: *Initiation*. Trans. from the German by John P.Robertson. London, George Allen & Unwin, 1965; Palo Alto (Calif.), Seed Center, 1974.

43 Guirdham, Arthur: *The Island*. Jersey, Neville Spearman, 1980.

44 Desjardins, Denise: *De Naissance en Naissance*.

Témoignage sur une vie antérieure. Paris, La Table Ronde, 1977.

45   Desjardins, Arnaud: *A la Recherche du Soi* II: *Le Vedanta et l'Inconscient.* Paris, La Table Ronde, 1978. See especially Chapter 4.

46   Desjardins, Denise: *La Mémoire des Vies Antérieures.* Ascèse et Vies successives. Paris, La Table Ronde, 1980.

47   Ib., p.134.

48   Ib., pp.148—160.

49   Ib., p.354.

50   Bernstein, Morey: *The Search for Bridey Murphy.* New York, Doubleday 1956.

51   Cerminara, Ref.65, Chap.2.

52   Pisani, Isola: *Mourir n'est pas Mourir.* Mémoires de vies antérieures. Paris, Robert Laffont, 1978.

53   Pisani, Isola: in Alaux's article, Ref.27.

54   Fiore, Edith: *You Have Been Here Before.* A Psychologist Looks at Past Lives. London, Sphere Books, 1980.

55   Wambach, Ref. 57, pp.62—66.

56   Iverson, Jeffrey: *More Lives than One.* London, Pan Books, 1977.
   However, most of the recalls that Iverson presents, unusual in their wealth of detail and inclusion of persons known to historians, are from a single subject, Jane Evans. It has now been shown convincingly (see Ian Wilson: *Reincarnation?* Penguin Books, 1982. Special Postscript) that three of Jane Evans' recalls are based on certain historical novels, and the one about the massacre of Jews may well be similarly derived. Such material can quite unconsciously be built up into a fantasy life. Hypnotic regression experiments must be designed with great care and awareness of pitfalls to be of any value.

57 Wambach, Helen: *Reliving Past Lives*: The Evidence Under Hypnosis. London, Arrow Books, 1980.

58 Ref.59, p.8.

59 Wambach, Helen: *Life Before Life*. New York, Bantam Books, 1979.

59a It is only fair to point out that certain dangers have been reported in amateur experiments in hypnotic regression and one should not plunge into it recklessly without knowing how to guard against them.

60 Guirdham, Arthur: *The Cathars and Reincarnation*. London, Neville Spearman, 1970.

61 Oldenbourg, Zoé: *Le Bûcher de Montségur*. Paris, Gallimard, 1959, pp.340–344.

61a Guirdham, Arthur: *We Are One Another*. Jersey, Neville Spearman, 1974. pp.222–223.

61b Guirdham, Arthur: *The Lake and the Castle*. Jersey, Neville Spearman, 1976. pp.415–419.

62 Guirdham, Ref.43, pp.92 and 102.

63 *The Middle Way*, *48*, 75–78, 1973.

64 Cerminara, Gina: *Many Mansions*. London, Neville Spearman, 1967.

65 Cerminara, Gina: *The World Within*. London, C.W. Daniel, 1973.

66 See Bernstein, Ref.50, III.3.

67 His Holiness Tenzin Gyatso: *The Opening of the Wisdom-Eye* and the History of the Advancement of Buddhadharma in Tibet. Madras, Theosophical Publishing House, 1971. pp.22–30.

67a Since this essay was written, a new translation of the book by the Dalai Lama (see note 67) has appeared: *Opening the Eye of New Awareness*, translated by Donald S. Lopez with Jeffrey Hopkins, London, Wisdom Publications, 1985. Though this version is much closer to the original Tibetan, my criticisms are essentially unaffected.

68 Thubten Zopa: *The Wish-fulfilling Golden Sun of the*

Mahāyāna Thought Training, Directing in the Short-cut Path to Enlightenment. Kathmandu, International Mahayana Institute; Eudlo (Qld.), Chenrezig Inst., 1975. pp. 1–2.

69   (LG): Losang Gyatso (bLo bzang rgya mtsho): *Srid zhi'i 'khrul 'khor 'byed pa'i legs bshad 'phrul gyi lde mig ces bya ba las stod cha, sngon dang phyi ma'i mtha' brtag pa'i rigs pa'i mdzod ces bya ba.* (The Magic Key of Elegant Sayings Opening the Mechanism of *Saṃsāra* and *Nirvāṇa*, Part I: A Treasury of Reasoning Analyzing the Past and Future.) Dharamsala, 1977.

70   Spencer-Brown, George: *Laws of Form*. New York, E.P. Dutton, 1979. pp.xix–xx.

71   Phur bu lcog Byams pa rgya mtsho: *Tshad ma'i gzhung don 'byed pa'i bsdus grva'i rnam bzhag Rigs lam 'phrul gyi lde mig ces bya ba las, Rigs lam chung ngu'i rnam par bshad pa.* Chap. 5, section 2.

72   The *Mahā-prajñāpāramitā-śāstra* quotes and refutes the personalist theory of a subtle body as ātman. Transln: Etienne Lamotte: *Le Traité de la Grande Vertu de Sagesse de Nāgārjuna*, Tome II. Louvain, Institut Orientaliste, 1949. p.744.

73   One reason for postulating an indestructible wind as well as an indestructible mind is so that they can act as each other's dominant condition.

74   Phur bu lcog Byams pa rgya mtsho: Ref.71, *Rigs lam 'bring gi skor*, Chap.4, section 2, part 2.

75   Dharmakīrti: *Pramāṇa-vārttika-kārikā*, II.38a-c.

76   Duddington, C.L.: *The Living World*. London, Arthur Barker, 1968. p.14.

77   Unless they extend the idea to mammals such as mice.

78   rGyal tshab rJe: *rNam 'grel thar lam gsal byed*, Chap.II. Sarnath, Pleasure of Elegant Sayings Printing Press, 1974. p.254.12.

79 St. Anselm: *The Ontological Proof of St. Anselm.* In Wolff, op.cit.Ref.21, p.100.

80 Ref.67, p.26.

81 Ref.78, p.252.

82 Candrakīrti: *Madhyamakāvatāra.* Ed. L.de la Vallée Poussin, p.208.

83 Lenin, V.I.: *Socialism and Religion* (1905). Transln in: K.Marx, F.Engels & V.Lenin: *On Historical Material-ism.* New York, International Publishers, 1974. pp.411–414.

84 Randall, Ref.89, p.21.

85 e.g. Smith, John Maynard: *The Theory of Evolution.* Penguin Books.

86 Monod, Jacques: *Chance and Necessity.* Transl. Austryn Wainhouse. London, Fontana Books, 1974.

87 Merrell-Wolff, Franklin: *The Philosophy of Con-sciousness Without an Object.* Reflections on the Nature of Transcendental Consciousness. New York, Julian Press, 1973. p.12.

88 Rose, Steven: *The Conscious Brain.* Penguin Books, 1976. p.365.

89 Randall, John L.: *Parapsychology and the Nature of Life.* London, Abacus, 1977.

90 Ref.87, p.11. 1896 is when Becquerel discovered the radioactive disintegration of uranium.

91 LeShan, L.: *The Medium, the Mystic, and the Phy-sicist.* London, Turnstone, 1974.

92 Charon, Jean E.: *L'Esprit, cet inconnu.* Verviers (Belgium), Marabout, 1977. According to his theory (p.151), each electron in the body would remember its own set of past existences.

93 James, William: *The Will to Believe.* In Wolff, op.cit. Ref.21, p.470.

94 Rose, Ref.88, p.364.

95 Schrödinger, Erwin: *What is Life?* and, *Mind and Matter.* Cambridge, Univ. Press, 1967. pp.126–137.

96   Spinoza, B.: *Ethics*, Pt.III, prop.2. Quoted by Schrö-
      dinger.

97   Monod, Ref.86, p.148.

98   Merrell-Wolff, Ref.87, p.151.

99   Or, as happened last week, a bus is driving through
      Lausanne when a crane collapses on it, killing seven
      people. Who would seriously claim that since the
      victims must have created the karma for such a
      death, it is pointless to seek the physical cause of
      this accident, or that no responsibility attaches to
      whoever may have been negligent in maintaining
      the crane?

100   e.g. Story's essay "Rebirth and the Western Think-
      er" (Ref.29, pp.30—45) contains several blunders.

101   See also Koestler, Arthur: *The Roots of Coincidence*.
      London, Picador, 1974. Chap.3, "Seriality and Syn-
      chronicity".

102   Monod, Ref.86, pp.111—112.

103   *Mi la'i mgur 'bum* (*The Hundred Thousand Songs of
      Milarepa*), Chap.3, p.18a.

104   Story, Ref.29, pp.210—212.

105   Ib., pp.208—9.

106   Nelli, René: *La Philosophie du Catharisme*. Paris,
      Payot, 1978. pp.183—4.

107   Pisani, Ref.52, pp.194—7 & 202—6.

108   Ib., p.179.

109   Story, Ref.29, pp.252—9.

110   Haich, Ref.42, p.336.

111   Grant, Ref.36, Pt.IV, Chap.2—6.

112   Ib., Pt.VI, Chap.7.

113   Cerminara, Ref. 64, p.29.

114   Ib., p.148.

115   We assume that Wambach's subjects are more or
      less typical of the human race as a whole. While
      people of different countries must differ somewhat
      in their past-life histories, and conceivably people

with more previous human existences might be more likely to take part in such experiments, one cannot reasonably suppose either that the subjects are a race apart among Americans or that Americans are the only people on Earth who have mostly avoided being animals or worse throughout the last four millennia.

116 e.g. Rhodes, F.H.T.: *The Evolution of Life*. Penguin Books, 2nd ed., 1976.

117 Vickerman, Keith, & Francis E.G. Cox: *The Protozoa*. John Murray, 1967.

118 Quoted by Murti, Ref.17, p.47.

119 e.g. Geshe Rabten: *The Preliminary Practices*. Dharamsala, Lib. Tib. Works and Archives, 1974. p.37.

120 Bareau, André: *Les Sectes Bouddhiques du Petit Véhicule*. Paris, Ecole Française d'Extrême-Orient, 1955. p.291, etc.

121 La Vallée Poussin, L.de: *L'Abhidharmakośa* de Vasubandhu. Mélanges Chinois et Bouddhiques, Vol.-XVI, Tome II, p.32 n.1.

122 Bhadantācariya Buddhaghosa: *The Path of Purification*. Transl. Bhikkhu Ñyāṇamoli. Boulder, Shambhala, 1976. XIX.22−23.

123 *Pratītyasamutpāda-hṛidaya*, 5.

124 *Prasannapadā*, 544.5.

125 Lamotte, Ref.72, p.745.

126 Ref.121, pp.31−57.

127 *Le Compendium de la Superdoctrine (Philosophie) (Abhidharma-samuccaya)* d' Asaṅga. Transl. Walpola Rahula. Paris, Ecole Française d'Extrême-Orient, 1971. p.68.

128 rJe Tsong kha pa: *Byang chub lam rim che ba*. Dharamsala ed., pp.159a−162a.

129 La Vallée Poussin, Ref.121, p.37 n.1.

130 *Abhidharmakośa*, III.13−15.

131 All this paragraph after Ref.126.

132   Wambach, Ref.57 & p.26 of Ref.59.

133   Ref.59, pp.173 & 176.

134   Story, Ref.29, pp.275−6.

135   Ib., p.192.

136   Ref.121, p.48 and n.2.

137   Ref.128, p.160a5.

138   Wambach, Ref.59, Chap. V. Here one can expect some bias in that people seeking spiritual growth would be more likely to participate.

139   Cerminara, Ref.64, pp.201, 202.

140   Wambach, Ref.59, Chap.VI.

141   Story, Ref.29, pp.183−190.

Quotations from sources not in English are translated by M.Willson unless otherwise indicated above. References 28 or 29, 46, 57 and 64 constitute the essential reading on the evidence for rebirth.

Wisdom Publications

Wisdom is a publisher of books on Buddhism and other spiritual and philosophical traditions.

Wisdom Theory-and-Practice Books
Bearing in mind that Buddhism is a living philosophy — something to learn and put into practice — we publish our theory-and-practice titles in three broad categories.

Basic Books: Orange Series
Intermediate Books: White Series
Advanced Books: Blue Series

These categories indicate the general level of approach of each title, whether sutra or tantra, and are thus a practical guide for readers in their choice of the most appropriate books.

Wisdom East-West Books: Grey Series
This new series of titles reflects the heartfelt desire current in the West to build bridges between the great philosophies and religions of the world and to explore the universality of their methods and ideas.

Wisdom Tibet Books: Yellow Series
There is growing worldwide interest in the Dalai Lama and Tibet. In this new series we will publish titles that show the history and culture — both before and after the Chinese conquest of 1959 — of this remarkable Buddhist country.

Please write to us at 23 Dering Street, London W1, England if you would like a copy of our catalogue of books, posters, prints, cards and audio and video tapes.